Praise for

How Does God Spell Community?

"Armin and I first met a few years ago when he joined our weekly Clarkston prayer meeting. Of course, we got to know each other at a deeper level as we prayed for each other's needs and concerns, and we became friends. It is exciting to see this book come to fruition as an answer to prayer.

"I saw Armin from a different perspective when he attended Clarkston Bible institute 2019–2020. Armin was a serious student, and it was exciting to see him grow in Christian maturity through the life-on-life discipleship that occurred through Clarkston Bible Institute.

"Colleen also attended some of the classes with Armin, and that was my major introduction to her. Since that time, we have gotten better acquainted as a result of working together doing training projects.

"I encourage you to read this book to see how important community has been in their spiritual growth and will be in yours as well."

—Terry D. Sparks
Executive Director
Clarkston Bible Institute

How Does God
Spell Community?

How Does God
Spell Community?

"LOL"—Life-On-Life

Armin and Colleen McMahan

BOOKLOGIX®
Alpharetta, GA

The authors have tried to recreate events, locations, and conversations from their memories of them. In some instances, in order to maintain their anonymity, the authors have changed the names of individuals and places. They may also have changed some identifying characteristics and details such as physical attributes, occupations, and places of residence.

ISBN: 978-1-6653-0460-3 - Paperback
eISBN: 978-1-6653-0461-0 - eBook

⊗This paper meets the requirements of ANSI/NISO Z39.48-1992 (Permanence of Paper)

All Scripture quotations, unless otherwise indicated, are taken from the Holy Bible, New International Version®, NIV®. Copyright ©1973, 1978, 1984, 2011 by Biblica, Inc.® Used by permission of Zondervan. All rights reserved worldwide. www.zondervan.com. The "NIV" and "New International Version" are trademarks registered in the United States Patent and Trademark Office by Biblica, Inc.®

1 1 2 1 2 2

Contents

Foreword

O ur prayer is that, through this book, people will see the beauty of community on mission with God. Our hope is also to show the heart of God through the life experiences of a couple.

We must admit that the thought of putting our experiences to paper seemed like a daunting task. We tried before and failed. There are lots of people who have things to say and have tried to write books. We are hoping that somehow our words can make a difference for the Kingdom of God and to present the peace of God, which makes a difference. As we continued to prayerfully consider this, it became a story of how God could take an average couple like us and do something extraordinary.

God took our limited abilities and skills and used them for his glory. That is God's heart: God loves to transform people. To take people who are ordinary and uncomplicated and form them into something glorious. To take people who are dishonorable and shameful and turn them into something of great value and honor.

This is our story of that life transformation by working with God in community. God is in community with Himself (Father, Son, and Holy Spirit), so it is no surprise that we need community. We need it desperately. Man was not meant to be a lone ranger or an island unto himself.

We hope that these words will inspire, encourage, challenge, and show the love of Christ that profoundly changes the world. This book is not meant to be a biography or a self-help book. The world has plenty of those already. Our intention is to show the struggles and joys of ordinary people. Of ordinary people who love God. We also want to express how God is mighty and powerful enough to overcome any weaknesses and failures by living in community with Him and mankind.

1

Seeing God's Purpose

I (Armin) will start with my story.

Much of my childhood seems to be a blur. As a child, I was brought up in the church from an early age. I faithfully attended a United Methodist Church down the street from where I lived in Newark, Ohio. I visited that church almost every Sunday until I went to college. All those early years, my parents would drop off my brother and me but that was the extent of their involvement. My grandma, on the other hand, would always ask, "Did you go to church this week?" She was a regular attendee of church herself and was a strong force in making sure I stayed connected. Personally, it felt weird to just be dropped off at church.

I talked with my parents about going to church, but they had no interest in participating. My mother grew up going to church, but she became disillusioned with the hypocrisy she saw and later wanted nothing to do with it. My dad followed suit as he was afraid to lose Mom due to her indifference about church. It was somewhat lonely going to church with my brother and not having my parents right beside me. Although I had some mentors and friends at church, I longed for the day that my parents could worship the Lord with me. As the years went by, I found myself going to Sunday school, Sunday service, and eventually, youth group. The idea of having my parents attend church with me was a long-lost memory.

Over the years I had been exposed to stories and Christian

teachings about God, but there never seemed to be any life transformation. I did not pray or read the Bible much outside of church. It seemed as if I was going to church because it was the thing to do on Sunday. There was not a lot of spiritual growth. I knew about Jesus but lacked that personal relationship with Him. There seemed to be a disconnect from what I was learning at church on Sunday and how I lived my life throughout the week. Many of the things that I did during the church service seemed to be more like activities than worshipping God. This is not to say that God did not use these things, but at the time I got lost in doing something to try and reach God. I had somehow missed the heart message. Doing what I thought was good seemed to be my focus of how to reach or please God.

Up to this point, my idea of living the Christian life was to do the right thing and avoid doing the wrong thing. I had a burden to try and do the right thing. This self-righteous attitude deceived me into thinking I was right with God. I was always under the presumption that if I did something wrong, I would be the guy who would get caught. I felt like I was under a microscope. The fear of getting caught became my way to escape sinning. It also did something more insidious: it set me up for a life of not taking any risks. If failure was an option, I wanted no part of it. I had no intention of engaging life for fear of failure. Fear of failure led me to be passive. This also led to a fear of rejection by others. The Bible talks a great deal about fear and fear is one of the most re-ferred-to subjects in the Bible. Time and time again, God's charge was to "fear not."

That was my life. Do good. Go to church. Go home. Go to school. Start all over again. I was constantly on the move but never getting anywhere. I often felt lonely and out of place. I quickly became a spectator trying to avoid a life of sin. I was afraid to sin. I believed God was harsh and wanted to squash me every time I failed.

I felt frustrated and it became a thing of bondage. I kept telling myself that following the rules was the ticket. Even though I followed the rules, sin had a way of creeping up on me. My thoughts and actions were not always pure. I tried to hide them, but many times my actions gave me away. This inconsistency was hard to deal with and caused a lot of anxiety.

At the time, I did not realize how my personal sin affected me or others around me. I seemed totally unaware of how my sin would affect my relationships with others and God. I would later discover that, even after being saved, the world of just following rules and regulations is not a very satisfying life. Following the rules would not profoundly change my behavior, but for whatever reason, I could not grasp that idea. Inside and outside, I was a mess. I stubbornly believed that following the rule of law was the most important thing as I grew up in the church. "Do the right thing" became my battle cry.

However, my battle cry often betrayed me. I was doomed to fail with this mind-set, as my view of God was incomplete and was not an accurate portrayal of the true character of God. As I continued to live this life, it became apparent that something was missing. I tried my best to be good. I followed the rules and the Ten Commandments. I was not hurting anyone. I felt I was right with God as I was not a troublemaker and had not broken any major commandments. However, I still fell short. I was hurting myself and others but refused to acknowledge it. What else could there be?

At age seventeen, I attended confirmation classes in the church. I guess you could say I was a late bloomer. Confirmation classes consisted of learning about the Christian faith and Christian doctrine in more detail. I started to understand a little more about faith and wanted to know more. As the other kids who took the classes were a bit younger than me, it was quite awkward. I did have trouble relating to them due to the age difference, but I faithfully read and examined the scriptures.

As a group, we learned about communion and baptism. Baptism caught my attention, and I was challenged by the act of baptism and what it meant. Was I living a transformed life or was something deeply missing? The answer was obvious. As I continued to study more about baptism, I started to see a connection or identification with Jesus through baptism. Looking at baptism drove me to discover that Jesus was what I needed to believe in. I knew baptism did not save me but this connection with Jesus was the thing that I had been looking for.

What I was looking for was found in what Jesus did for humanity and for me. He did the one thing I could not do. I could not save myself or change myself in my own power. I had tried so many times to change my behavior that I felt like a complete failure. My good works fell short, and my heart was not right. Forgiveness was found in Jesus and Jesus alone.

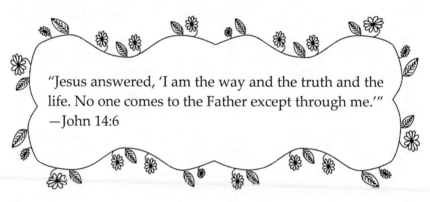

"Jesus answered, 'I am the way and the truth and the life. No one comes to the Father except through me.'"
—John 14:6

I also realized that He cleansed me of my sins.

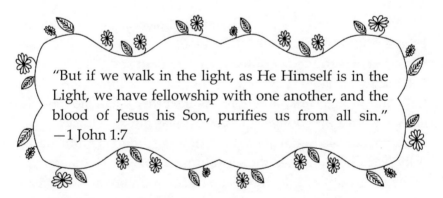

"But if we walk in the light, as He Himself is in the Light, we have fellowship with one another, and the blood of Jesus his Son, purifies us from all sin."
—1 John 1:7

This Good News was not just for me, but for everyone. I put my faith and trust in Jesus and that His grace (God's Riches At Christ's Expense) was enough.

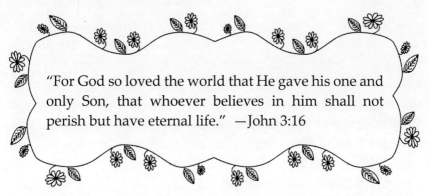

"For God so loved the world that He gave his one and only Son, that whoever believes in him shall not perish but have eternal life." —John 3:16

I also acknowledged that I was a sinner and wanted to turn away from that lifestyle. I felt a peace that I was reconciled to the one who created me. I knew salvation was by grace and that I had nothing to do with it.

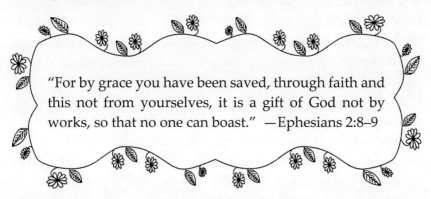

"For by grace you have been saved, through faith and this not from yourselves, it is a gift of God not by works, so that no one can boast." —Ephesians 2:8–9

This gift of God impacted me in a way that would lead me on a journey to become more like Christ.

I was baptized shortly after that. I remember like it was yesterday coming out of the water feeling cleansed. I knew that I was somehow changed. My past did not seem to hold me hostage and my future looked a whole lot brighter. This was just the beginning in a long journey that would be filled with many ups and downs.

At this point, I realized that God would be with me despite any difficulties that I would face. I graduated high school and off to college I went. I was hoping to save the world with my newfound faith and trust in Jesus. I was different and I wanted everyone to know it.

I attended the Ohio State University branch in Newark, Ohio, and was able to connect with some believers. I was also able to join a good Bible study. I enjoyed that fellowship and was even able to hang out with a guy from the Navigators. The Navigators is a ministry that shares the Gospel of Jesus Christ as well as helps Christians grow in their personal relationship with Jesus. This Navigator missionary helped me to begin looking at the Bible as my compass. This helped me to gain a better understanding of the world and how I could relate to it.

Things were going well, and then I had to transfer to the Ohio State University main campus in Columbus, Ohio. Immediately, I encountered a new problem: it was making connections with other believers. As big as Ohio State was, I thought this would not be a problem. Boy was I wrong. I soon felt like a complete outcast. I also felt as if I had stepped into another dimension. The university was remarkably diverse, and most ethnicities were represented in the school population. It was a city within a city. I tried to connect with others, but it did not go well. I had a lot to learn. It seemed as if no one cared.

Connecting with others was much more difficult than I had anticipated. I knew I was different but much of the college world seemed to be going in the opposite direction. I attended a Bible study and the group started talking about aliens and all kinds of weird stuff. It gave me an unpleasant feeling, a sense that something was not right. It was time to get out of Dodge. There was drinking everywhere and all kinds of stuff going on which I dare not even mention. If you did not drink, you were out. It was as simple as that.

Even though I was thinking differently, my intention was still to avoid sin. I lacked a more complete understanding of my identity in Christ and His great depth of love for me. I moved further away from reading the Bible, relying on the Holy Spirit, prayer, and Christian community. I soon found myself so isolated that I started living at the library to avoid others and sin. I was miserable as isolation was driving me away from people. I was still caught in the trap of avoiding sin as a way of reaching God.

As I was exposed to more and more of the campus lifestyle, I became more discouraged. I was not yet strong enough in Christ to avoid temptation. I finally gave in. One night, I got so drunk that I am not sure how I even made it home. I do not remember a lot about that night. I do remember someone saying, "Here comes the police, prop him up." When I finally got back to my apartment, I looked in the mirror and saw my shirt was hanging out and filthy. I looked awful and felt awful. I could have very easily ended up in jail that night. I felt horrible for three days afterward. I felt like a fog was hanging over me. Never again, I said. That did not stop me from drinking at the time, but by the grace of God, I never came close to losing control as I did that night.

Unfortunately, I also fell into the trap of pornography. A small peek was all it took. It went from a small peek to a lot more. It seemed harmless at first, but I was soon off to the races. I rationalized it in my mind by saying I was not having sex with anyone. I was merely looking at an image. I later found out that images are especially important as we are made in the image of God. The kind of image we present to others and to God is particularly important. God is calling us to be an image-bearer. Even though it was behind closed doors, I knew it was wrong. Despite trying to hide it from others, I could not hide it from God. To Him, I am an open book.

Later I realized that by getting away from the Bible, prayer, the Holy Spirit, and Christian community, I had unknowingly let Satan have a foothold. I had allowed the things of the world to overtake me and chew me up. I had gotten so far away from God that I began to wonder how He could ever take me back. I had disgraced God with my lack of devotion and then by my lack of concern to keep myself from sinning. It was almost too much to bear. I somehow made it through college and graduated, sins and all. It was not a time that I like to reminisce about. What had started out as zeal to save the world had turned into a disaster. It was a dark time in my life. Even so, God was teaching me some valuable lessons.

After graduating I went back home with my parents. The Word of God and the Holy Spirit started to reveal to me more and more about how I had been living and that it was contrary to God's ways.

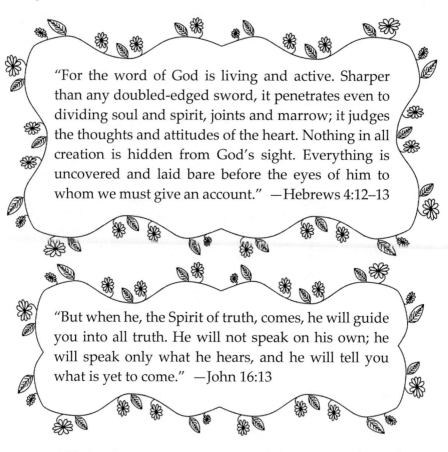

"For the word of God is living and active. Sharper than any doubled-edged sword, it penetrates even to dividing soul and spirit, joints and marrow; it judges the thoughts and attitudes of the heart. Nothing in all creation is hidden from God's sight. Everything is uncovered and laid bare before the eyes of him to whom we must give an account." —Hebrews 4:12–13

"But when he, the Spirit of truth, comes, he will guide you into all truth. He will not speak on his own; he will speak only what he hears, and he will tell you what is yet to come." —John 16:13

Going home provided an environment where I could reassess what had happened. I confessed the things that had severely damaged my testimony and relationship with God. I had become distracted by worldly things and the pleasures of life. I had put myself in a place that I did not want to go. I had failed God; however, I did sense that He was not going to fail me. As I turned away from my sins, I started to really embrace the idea of forgiveness. I wanted to live a transformed life. It was a process and certainly did not happen overnight; however, I was moving forward with His help.

My first agenda was to find a job. I had graduated with a bachelor of arts in psychology. I found it difficult trying to find a job using my degree. I felt like I looked under every rock for something related to my degree. It was quite depressing. So depressing that I started to doubt myself. Again, my identity was not firm in Christ as my provider. However, God was faithful in providing work, it just was not what I expected.

Since any income is better than no income, I started a job cleaning several buildings. When you are starting at ground zero, even a small job can be fulfilling. I cleaned several buildings by sweeping floors and scrubbing toilets. Just what I wanted to do with my degree. I started out at $3.35 an hour; I thought I hit the mother lode. I worked hard and did my best even though it was not what I wanted to do. I did my best not to complain or feel devalued. It was as if God began to instill in me that my identity could not be related to any job. My identity was beginning to shift.

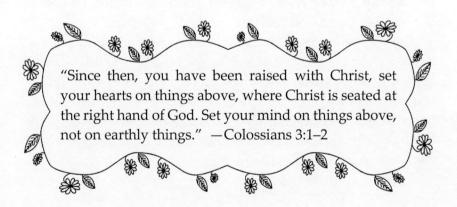

"Since then, you have been raised with Christ, set your hearts on things above, where Christ is seated at the right hand of God. Set your mind on things above, not on earthly things." —Colossians 3:1–2

I knew that God was working for me and in me. I was so thankful. Since then, I have never related my identity to any job. Jobs will come and go. Besides, I had seen so many people get crushed by losing a job. I wanted no part of that. I was just thankful that I had found work.

I was finally able to find a job related to my degree working at a hospital in a chemical dependency unit. I seemed to be on my way. I learned a lot about alcohol and substance addiction, mainly from the medical model perspective. I took patients' vital signs (temperature, blood pressure, and breathing status) to check their recovery process. I also facilitated group discussions about recovery issues and relapse prevention. I attended Alcoholics Anonymous (AA) meetings with the patients and became familiar with the twelve steps used in recovery. I was able to buy my first car and save $5,000. I did not have any hobbies other than tennis and bowling, so it was easy to save. At the time, I did not have any other bills. Things were looking up.

I should have known that trouble was lying around the corner. Due to some insecurities and bad judgment on my part, I was asked to resign. At first, I felt terrible. I had allowed myself to cross boundaries and misread people. I felt bad and I should have. I felt guilty. It took some time, but I again confessed my sin and turned away from it. I gave the situation to the Lord. I knew that God was good and that my response should not be to complain or grumble. I was the one who had put myself at risk as well as the lives of others. God had nothing to do with that.

The consequences of losing that job were hard, but a much-needed piece in restoring myself to the Lord and to others that I had let down. I vowed that I would be much more careful next time and that I would become a person of integrity. I somehow knew God would be faithful and get me through it. That is the beauty of God. He is faithful, all the time, to do what is best and right. His Word is totally trustworthy.

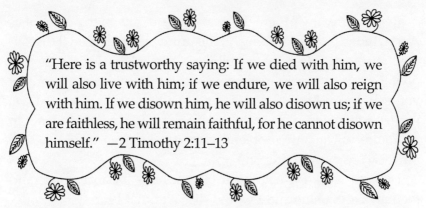

"Here is a trustworthy saying: If we died with him, we will also live with him; if we endure, we will also reign with him. If we disown him, he will also disown us; if we are faithless, he will remain faithful, for he cannot disown himself." —2 Timothy 2:11–13

Despite my willful disobedience (sin), God was faithful and allowed me to start working at another hospital. I was completely honest with my new employer about my last place of employment. It was by God's grace that they decided to hire me anyway. I worked there for the next two years. It was difficult work at times, but I could not complain.

As a treatment aid, I took vital signs for those who were detoxing from alcohol and/or drugs. It was tough to see people suffer greatly for three to five days while coming off drugs/alcohol. Others had longer and more complicated detoxes because of their heavy use. Some almost died. I began to see the long-term damage from alcohol and drug dependency. I later heard stories about others who had gone through the detox program and later died because of their addiction. Fortunately, I had a couple of great Christian nurses who worked with me and encouraged me along the way despite the difficulties.

At the same hospital, I later transitioned to a new position of detox counselor. I showed films about recovery and led a small group. I did have some difficulties in relating to the patients and some of the staff. Many of the staff and others would often say, "Armin, you are never going to understand addicts/alcoholics because you've never been one." They were right. I could not understand how the mind of an addict or alcoholic works. I did understand that addicts/alcoholics can be forgiven. I did understand that forgiveness was offered to all. I also understood that Christ was the difference-maker.

In many treatment centers, recovery is based on the Alcoholics Anonymous (AA) program and the principles espoused. I discovered that AA was built on biblical principles. Using a higher power than yourself to stay sober, learning how to forgive yourself and others, and making amends to those harmed are particularly good principles to live by. It was also done in community. The only problem seemed to be what type of higher power were they relying on?

I would work for nearly thirty years in substance abuse and mental health fields and I would discover that I rarely saw long-term sobriety apart from God. For those who were transformed, they no longer lived the life of an addict or an alcoholic. Jesus was the basis of their recovery. I know that many might want to debate me on this issue, but this is what I have personally observed by watching those who have maintained long-term sobriety. No longer an addict/alcoholic but transformed by Christ. No longer desiring to drink or use drugs. Their identity was in being a new creation, not in a substance. They truly were a new creation once Christ came into their lives. They were no longer the same.

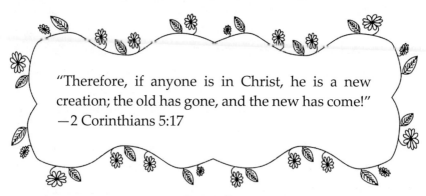

"Therefore, if anyone is in Christ, he is a new creation; the old has gone, and the new has come!"
—2 Corinthians 5:17

God gives us an imagination. In many, this imagination has been shut off. When that happens, it is impossible to see that change is possible. As the failures continue to mount, the possibility of changing slips away. When a person is a new creation, the future looks so much brighter. Imagination now allows for a change that was once impossible by human effort.

As I continued working in the hospital, I began to wonder about my career options. Do I become a certified counselor? Do I change directions? As I pondered these questions, I started to date Colleen McWilliams. The questions subsided for the moment as my attention was elsewhere.

Colleen and I connected on a different level and soon started to date more frequently. We both loved and believed in God. Both of us had turned to Jesus as our source of salvation. We both wanted to positively influence the world with our faith. As I continued working at the hospital, we became engaged in the summer of 1990 and were married in April 1991.

Colleen's story is next.

2

Mission Calling, Colleen's Story

I moved many times as a young child. Mom and Dad alternated moving from central to southern Ohio. My parents would move wherever the job market took them. It was hard to make friends with all the moving. I was not able to establish many long-lasting relationships except for one.

When I was in fourth grade, I moved back to a small country community in north-central Ohio. This is when I reconnected with my friend from my early days. We became super close, almost inseparable. We enjoyed hanging out and doing things together. Our families were awfully close, so we were more like blood relatives. We camped and went to church activities together. She was the sister I never had.

As both my parents had to start working full time to make ends meet, my priorities started to shift. I joined 4-H and marching band in elementary school to keep out of trouble and to have something to do. I would continue serving in 4-H and marching band through my high school years; 4-H and band became more than just a way to keep myself out of trouble. Serving in 4-H and band taught me a lot about leadership skills and how to effectively work with others. I enjoyed working on projects and building relationships.

On a spiritual level, I was exposed to many different expressions of worship in the Lutheran church. Worship included casual playing of guitars, singing around campfires, formal high church liturgy, playing pipe organs, and singing hymns. My mom's family immigrated to this country from eastern Europe and my mom instilled in me that family was extremely important.

When we visited my grandparents in Pennsylvania, we would go to church with my cousins and grandmother. My grandmother attended a Serbian Orthodox church where they sang and spoke the service in both Serbian and English. This church experience helped me to worship in a different culture. This helped me to understand that worshipping God expresses itself differently in other geographical areas.

My parents were regularly active in the life of the church, so I lived most of my life in or around the church. Going to church was as normal as going to school, so I saw the value they placed on participating and being a part of a body of believers. I went to Sunday school and youth group every Sunday unless I was sick. Mom and Dad refused to let my brother and me play hooky from church. I learned that going to church was especially important in the growth of a young person.

My junior year was set aside for going to confirmation classes. The confirmation classes consisted of reading Genesis, Exodus, the Kings of Israel, the Prophets, Matthew, Luke, Acts, and the Epistles. I learned church history, the difference between the law and the Gospel, and how to listen to the sermons and summarize a message. This gave me a good foundation for my faith, but I did not realize who Jesus was apart from God the Father. I did not know Jesus as God the Father. Much of the teaching about the Holy Spirit was lacking as well, so I had an incomplete picture of God.

In high school, I was involved in band and choir and became a staff member of the yearbook. I continued to be active in the church and in youth group. My youth leaders took my youth group to small conferences around the central Ohio area, and my outlook started to change.

The Lord began using other people to get my attention as He was preparing me to follow Him. My brother joined the navy when I was a sophomore. One day, my brother called home from overseas and he asked me a question: "How is your relationship with the Lord?" I had to think for a moment. No one ever asked about my relationship with God before. Up to this point, the focus had been on community worship and praising God. I did not have a personal relationship with Him, so I did not have an answer. I never forgot that question. That question led me on my journey to discover who Jesus is.

At age eighteen, I was praising the Lord in the liturgy part of the service. As I was singing, I heard the Lord say, "You are singing about Jesus my Son." Growing up I had learned about God, not necessarily about Jesus. I remembered that question, "How is your relationship with the Lord?" Something was missing but I could not quite put my finger on it. I started reading the Gospels and soon began to fall in love with Jesus. I began putting my trust and faith in Christ, not my knowledge of Him.

"But these are written that you may believe that Jesus is the Christ, the Son of God, and that by believing you may have life in his name." —John 20:31

During my senior year of high school, I received information and an application about a mission trip. I felt the Lord calling me to go, but I did not have the money. I was also looking at what I was going to do for a career. I had a choice to go to business school or go on a mission trip. In my heart, I knew which direction I should go, but I was not willing to go there. I did not have the money for either, but I decided to take out a loan and attend Bradford Business School in Columbus, Ohio. I knew that it was the wrong decision, but I made it anyway. I never asked God or my parents regarding this decision.

So, off to business school I went. After about four months, I realized working in accounting was not what I wanted to do for the rest of my life. However, I did finish school and received my associate degree in accounting.

God protected me during this time from many of the potential pitfalls of the campus lifestyle. I was young and naïve about worldly things. My roommates drank and smoked marijuana, so they did not invite me to their parties. I was okay with that. I would either go home or go to a friend's house on the weekends. One weekend, they had a party on the third floor of my apartment and my roommate was so drunk she fell off the balcony. She ruptured her spleen and broke several bones. She was fortunate to have survived, but she did have to drop out of school. I lost another roommate that weekend because she got in trouble for hosting the party that resulted in the infamous fall from the balcony.

I stayed away from drinking because alcohol negatively affected my cousins and family. My roommates' shenanigans only reinforced that alcohol was bad news. I did not drink but that did not stop me from socializing with others.

I left another party to visit with one of my friends. She made a pass at me, and it totally took me by surprise. Then she started to physically touch me, and I did not know what to do. I should have resisted her invitation, but I did not. Afterward, my spirit was crushed, and I was angry with her since she was a trusted friend. My anger turned into rage as I felt cheated. My anger was not necessarily aimed at her but at Satan and his minions.

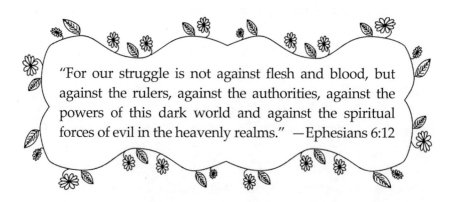

"For our struggle is not against flesh and blood, but against the rulers, against the authorities, against the powers of this dark world and against the spiritual forces of evil in the heavenly realms." —Ephesians 6:12

I moved back home for a time and commuted to school and work. During this time, I spent a lot of time in the book of Psalms and crying out to God. I was able to forgive my friend but forgiving myself was a lot harder. I blamed myself for not resisting the temptation of sexual desire. I started journaling my thoughts and feelings. As I read the Bible, healing occurred as God spoke Truth to me. I was a child of His who was hurting and needed for-giveness. Christ's forgiveness overcame my shame and disobedi-ence. As I continued to read Psalm 18, I was comforted by God's mercy and that I could take refuge in His wings as I faced this storm.

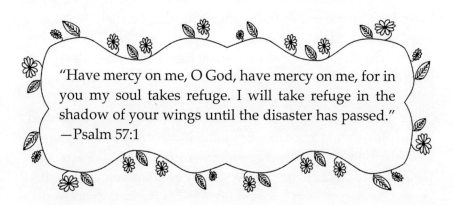

"Have mercy on me, O God, have mercy on me, for in you my soul takes refuge. I will take refuge in the shadow of your wings until the disaster has passed."
—Psalm 57:1

I was vulnerable and could have very easily strayed away from God completely, but He was faithful to keep me from remaining on a path that would have harmed me more. He was not only my Savior but my protector as well.

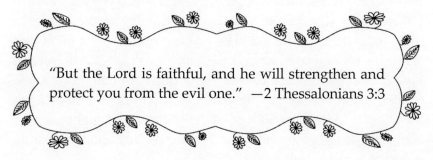

"But the Lord is faithful, and he will strengthen and protect you from the evil one." —2 Thessalonians 3:3

As I moved forward from this trial, I was encouraged and strengthened that God would walk with me during my time of trouble. I believed that He alone had the answers and power to allow me to heal. By faith, I had to believe that God was good, and He had my best interest at heart.

While going to school, I worshipped at the Lutheran Student Chapel at the Ohio State University. I began making friends and became involved in the Lutheran Student Movement. The Lutheran Student Movement is a student-led organization that is self-governed for the Lutheran campus ministry.

God, in His great mercy and compassion, allowed me to find my way to a community despite my disobedience. Because of my newfound connections, I was asked to become the Great Lakes International Secretary. I agreed despite not knowing exactly what I was doing. As an international secretary, I documented interactions with the international students and invited them to the Lutheran Chapel on campus at the Ohio State University.

I began to meet a lot of international students. I served them by helping them to become acquainted with American culture. I also attended international activities which helped me learn about their cultures. This helped me to consider other people's cultural perspectives. This was my first brush with the international idea which would come up later. Afterward, I talked to the congregation about my contacts with the internationals.

While at a National Student Movement Conference, I picked up a flyer for a youth ministry opportunity with Lutheran Youth Encounter. I filled out the application and was accepted. I flew to California to start youth ministry 101 training at the Lutheran Bible Institute. As I trained to be a youth minister, I learned that any ministry is relational, and not just a program. I also learned how crucial it would be to work with others in this process. We formed teams that shared the love of Christ in different areas of the US and abroad. It was a great experience that taught me a lot about building community and relying on one another despite different backgrounds, skills, and abilities.

That spring I went to Portland, Oregon, to assist three churches with administrative duties, visitation, developing a volunteer program, and discipling youth. While connecting with these churches I met rural, suburban, and inner-city youth. This experience allowed me to view a wide range of different dynamics and complexities regarding socioeconomic and cultural differences within the youth culture.

After completing my internship in Portland, the beautiful Black Hills of South Dakota were my next stop in continuing my education in youth ministry. I attended Lee Valley Ranch, which was the hands-on training site for developing youth leaders. At the ranch, I learned how to set goals, evangelize, work on team-building activities, and create a vision cast for building youth discipleship.

During this process, several teams lived in communities doing life-on-life. We worked together doing service projects, kitchen patrol, camp chores, and team-building activities. This helped our team to build trust and unity. I also learned how to develop a quiet time by spending quality time alone with the Lord daily.

Part of my training involved spending twenty hours in the wilderness by myself. I had to let go of my ability to control my environment because of the elements and potential threats from wildlife. I was at the mercy of the great outdoors. We did not have tents, so I slept on the ground in an open area. This reality helped me to trust God more and be completely dependent on Him.

After completing my training in South Dakota, I went back to my home congregation in Ohio and volunteered to teach confirmation class. I applied for and was hired as a part-time youth director at a local church in Newark, Ohio. During this time, my pastor would challenge me to pray out loud in group settings. This was such a foreign concept to me. It took quite some time to pray out loud. I had a lot of questions and negative thoughts. I felt very inadequate and that my prayers were very shallow. I often had difficulty speaking in public. This fear hindered my confidence and ability to pray in front of others. Finally, I started to pray aloud during one of the weekly staff meetings. It took time, but I soon began to feel more comfortable praying aloud. As I started to pray more, my confidence increased, and I became more comfortable praying within a church body. It helped that I was praying in a community where I felt safe.

While I was a youth director, I lived with an elderly lady who was a missionary. She discussed her missionary travels and had connections in Singapore and Malaysia. After her husband died, she continued to support missions abroad and she kept in touch with many of the missionaries that she had connected with in Asia. She inspired me and supported me to continue in ministry. She helped disciple me and grow my relationship with the Lord. I assisted her with organizing many of her presentations of her trips that she utilized to educate local churches about missions. As I helped her in this area it gave me insight about how a missionary operates and functions in the field.

While staying with my elderly missionary friend, I started dating Armin. As we continued to see each other, we started to discuss marriage. I was hoping to marry a pastor so that we could serve in ministry together. Armin had no desire to work with youth or be a pastor. I became profoundly disappointed with Armin's lack of desire to do either one. Still, the relationship continued, and we were married in April of 1991.

I continued to serve youth and became a nanny for a family who had three children. Working with kids came naturally and I began to think about having children. During our life together, Armin and I were blessed to have three wonderful children: Jalen, Seth, and Meghan. The Lord blessed Armin with a good job, so I was able to concentrate on raising our children.

After our first child was born, I started volunteering with youth and with children's ministry at church. Soon, Armin and I started to build our family by adding two more children to the mix. I started homeschooling our children as there was some concern about going to public school and how this would impact their faith. As our children became older, it became much more difficult to teach all of them as they were all about two years apart, Armin and I ended up putting them in public school, trusting that God would somehow work it out.

As time went on, I started to accept the idea that Armin and I would not necessarily work in ministry together. It was hard, but I never quite gave up on Armin. But as I continued to pray for Armin, I started to see that God was working in his life. He attended a seventy-two-hour retreat. After attending, I noticed a change in him. I was immensely proud of him and saw a glimpse of light that God was using him. Maybe we would serve in ministry together after all.

God began to open a door for Armin by allowing him to work at a local mental health agency and at a local jail. He was good at being a person of peace and provided a quiet spirit to those who were so terribly troubled. I believed that the Lord had called him to these jobs. The Lord was providing us with a steady income, great benefits, and a good retirement plan. I became extremely comfortable during the time Armin worked at the jail. However, he kept telling me that he would not retire there. I did not take that to heart. I heard it, but I truly did not believe what he was saying.

In 2008, Armin had a life-changing experience that would break his heart for the persecuted church and change the direction of our lives. That experience would eventually lead Armin on a path to quit his job and begin a process to becoming a full-time missionary. I struggled a lot with this transition. Transitions have always been tough for me, but God has grown me in this area.

Most of our lives had been focused on our children. We made a lot of mistakes in parenting. However, we wanted to have our children believe they were incredibly important, and that God loved them. We wanted them to know that Christ was the difference maker.

As our children grew up, we always attended church together. We also attended all their sporting events and other school related activities. We wanted them to know that we supported them and that we wanted to be a part of their life inside the church and outside the church. We would often take trips or do things together as a family. We were building memories that would last a lifetime.

As our children got older, we would often get compliments about how well-behaved they were. Armin would often say, "We did not have much to do with it, we made far too many mistakes. God was the one who did it." Armin gave credit where it was due. God is faithful. We knew God was working in our children's lives despite our shortcomings.

However, there were always questions as we moved forward. In 2012, I had more questions. Our local Alive Vineyard Church had developed a partnership with Brazil by planting churches. Our community church began forming a team to go to Brazil. I asked Armin if he wanted to go. I felt a calling to go but Armin prayed about it and did not feel called to go. I thought Armin would go with me. I asked Armin again about going. Again, he prayed about it and did not feel God had called him to go. I was very frustrated as I was certain God had called me. I wanted my husband to go with me too. Everyone in the church automatically thought that because I was going, Armin would also. Again, I thought about Armin and I doing ministry together. Why me? Why not Armin too? Armin continued to believe that he was not called to go.

However, he encouraged me to take a step of faith and go to Brazil. I took that leap of faith and traveled to Brazil without Armin. I traveled with a couple of members from the Alive Vineyard Church and members of the Delaware Vineyard Church.

As usual, I made several good contacts during the flight to Brazil and had some good spiritual discussions. Armin is always dumbfounded at how easily I connect with people while flying. God just seems to put people in my path who want to talk, especially on airplanes.

Our first flight went through Miami and then to Belem, Brazil. Our connecting flight to Altamira had left earlier in the day and we had missed it. The airport staff said it was our fault that we missed the flight. We felt that the airlines were at fault. Finally, the airline attendant at the ticket counter discovered a communication error. It was clearly not our fault.

As a result of this so-called communication error, we ended up stuck at the airport in Belém. No one on our team could speak Portuguese and at this juncture, we did not have an interpreter. We prayed that, somehow, we would overcome the language barrier and get our flights figured out. We were in a pickle and needed help at once. Shortly after praying, a man came to the counter who spoke both Portuguese and English. Just in time, "here came the calvary." He was wonderful and helped us in our time of need. Thank you, Jesus! We certainly needed help.

As the ticket agent started booking our next flight, the computer divided our party and placed each on different flights. One flight went to Altamira, Brazil, and the other one back to Miami. It took most of the evening to get us all on the same flight the next day. Instead of complaining, I thanked God for the infrastructure we have in the United States. I did not want to take anything for granted.

It was quite an ordeal, and the trip was just getting started. I was looking forward to getting out of the airport and finding a hotel in Belem. To our surprise, all the hotels in Belem were booked. We ended up spending the night at the airport. There were no benches or carpeting. That night we slept on the hard linoleum floor. I can only imagine what we looked like as seven Americans doing our best to get comfortable sleeping on our luggage. Trying to sleep at an airport is nerve-racking and we certainly were not in a sleeping mode. One eye open and one eye closed. It was a long night. The trip was beginning to sound more like a horror movie than a mission trip. I began to wonder what I had gotten myself into. I wondered if we would ever make it to our destination.

We finally made it to Altamira despite all the difficulties. When we arrived, we only had a few minutes to rearrange our luggage for a five-day boat trek on the Xingu River. We had to take a small truck to get to the boat. It reminded me of a cattle truck. There was not a lot of room. We all climbed in the truck and traveled the rain-washed roads of Brazil. Finally, we made it to the boat. From there it took us another nine hours to reach the first village. We were exhausted and needed God's help and encouragement.

One of our morning duties was to lead a devotion. Everyone was assigned a day to lead. The daily devotions helped set the tone for the day and helped us to focus on God and lean on His strength.

After our first devotion, we started our journey to visit four villages. At the first village, we offered Vacation Bible School (VBS) for the kids. The mothers of the children were able to help us with the VBS as they seemed so love-starved for company and affection.

One of the next villages was an indigenous reserve. We were not sure if we could travel there because of a rumor that the missionary who owned the boat had been poaching in the area. This missionary wanted to get to the village as soon as possible because the patriarch and pastor had just died. No one was currently shepherding the church. Despite the obstacle of the rumor, we were able to proceed without any difficulties. When we finally visited this village, it was at the end of the rainy season. We climbed down a ladder from the boat and waded in two feet of water on the dock. It was tricky, but by God's grace, we made it. Our team was able to pray for and strengthen the church despite the loss of their pastor. We also led worship, gave our testimonies, and prayed for those who wanted to believe in Christ.

We visited another village in which the matriarch wanted the mission team to help disciple her people. The boat docked and the children took us in with open arms. They were playing at the water's edge and jumped from the dock into the murky water surrounded by water lilies. The men of the team jumped in the water with the kids. They were having fun even though this area was known for having anacondas. They were fearless and played for hours.

Day-to-day activities never seemed to be boring. Even routine things were quite interesting. Bathroom accommodations were not the best as the toilet was what Brazilians refer to as a keyhole. Just a hole in the ground and nothing more. Bathing was always a fun adventure as it was in the creek. I never was sure who or what might be lurking in the shadows. I also found some fire ants that made the adventure even more interesting. Despite these inconveniences, life continued.

Traveling to the next village, we had to trek above the murky water on the dock. It was a long walk surrounded by water and lilies. I remember how afraid I was as I walked in the middle of the dock being careful not to get too close to the edge. I am not a big anaconda fan! I did not want to trip and fall into the water and become a snack. I was praying and concentrating on not falling in. When I hit solid ground, I sighed a big breath of relief and thanked God for my safety. However, walking back to the boat was a cinch as God took away the fear.

Next, we had to climb a steep hill to the community center. Once there, we played games with the kids and their mothers. We shared the Gospel of salvation using the colors of Christ made from a bracelet: red represented Jesus's blood, black stood for sin, blue depicted baptism, white portrayed the forgiveness of sins, green showed growth, and yellow described heaven. All these colors represented the complete story of the Gospel. The kids wore these bracelets every day to remind them about what Jesus did for them. They also wanted to share with others about how Jesus had saved them.

In the evening, the Brazilians wanted to have a worship service. To our surprise, the community center was packed. We praised God well into the night. During ministry time, a teen wanted to repent and believe in Christ. One of the national missionaries grabbed my arm and asked me to lead a prayer with her. I had never done anything like that before. I had prayed before but had never prayed to help someone find salvation. I fumbled over the words. I was thankful that an interpreter helped me. It was a good day for salvation, sharing with the people, and playing games.

Later, we went back to our boat and slept on hammocks (in Portuguese, it is called a *rede*) that hung from the rafters of the boat. The next day, we left that village and headed north. Since the Amazon was so close, we thought we would take a detour to sight-see. As we approached the Amazon River, the beautiful blue Xingu River started blending into the murky waters. As we floated into the Amazon, the men jumped off the boat. However, I could not get myself to dive in. Again, with anacondas in the water, diving in still did not appeal to me.

Traveling southward, we went toward Porto de Moz, Brazil. We took a couple of hours swimming where the waters were clearer and supposedly free of anacondas. As we were docking, I saw a military vessel coming toward us. One of the missionaries told us to get out our passports and not to talk. Immediately, apprehension and fear took over. Military officers with automatic weapons boarded the boat and questioned the owner. For a moment, tensions were extremely high, but God was gracious, and nothing came of it. The military personnel left with some instructions, and it was back to business as usual.

We continued to enjoy the beach and the water. A few went fishing and caught our dinner for the night. We arrived at Porta de Moz just as a storm was approaching. We stayed on the boat until the storm blew over. The lightning was fierce but majestic. It was beautiful as I watched from my hammock (*rede*). The waves, rain, and lightning were an incredible display of God's power. I had never seen a river with such high waves. In the moment, I almost forgot I was on a river boat.

After the storm passed, we went ashore and met with some Brazilians who knew our sons, Seth and Jalen. Jalen and Seth had been on a mission trip the year before and had visited that area. It was so good to connect with others who had seen our boys. It also felt good that our church from Newark, Ohio, was helping the people in this area.

As we met more people, we were becoming connected within the community. That evening we worshipped together, and I gave my testimony. I shared how the Lord had cared for me and walked beside me even as my father had died earlier in the year. During ministry time, the whole church came up for prayer which surprised me. I was not expecting the entire church to go up for prayer. Our responsibility as a team was to pray for each one as they came up. As I prayed, something did not seem right. Our team leader sensed the same thing. He came over and prayed that I would be bold. I became bolder with my prayers, and I started to see God move. God gave me the boldness that I could make a difference with my prayers. I noticed that many of the other team members were becoming bolder as well. God was moving in power and giving all of us more confidence.

As we were nearing the end of our trip, I began to think a lot, about several things: I wondered about the Unites States' influence on the Amazon culture. I noticed that many of the songs we sang were American worship songs but some of the Brazilians had started to write some songs from their own hearts. I also observed how technology had impacted the area. I noticed satellite dishes and generators in the primitive houses. The village was changing as the Brazilians now sat around in the evening watching TV. Also, the children had cell phones. They were snapping our photos and playing games on them. Technology had made its way into the rainforest and the community was changing.

My mind drifted to the beauty that surrounded me. I noticed the river dolphins swimming alongside the boat, the toucans flying and perching in the trees, the sloths hanging on the branches, and water buffaloes eating near the shore. I then saw a red-steel electric pole above the tree canopy. It seemed so out of place in the beauty of it all. Even though I marveled at the absolute allure of the jungle expanse, I also saw the influence from the outside coming into the jungle, untamed yet somehow marred by outside influences. It was a far-reaching thought.

On the last leg of our journey, we went inland. We walked through the rainforest to minister and pray for many people. In fact, we engaged an unreached people group of that area called the Asurini do Xingu People. We invited a lot of people to a church service as we went door to door. The church was packed with people and everyone participated. It was exciting and amazing to connect with so many others. As we were worshipping, we saw so many people that we had invited. This greatly encouraged and strengthened us. After the service, everyone from preschool to ninety years old played London Bridge. It was amazing to see everyone having so much fun in fellowship within a community. Our trip finally came to an end.

The flight back home was uneventful. I felt honored that the Lord chose the team to encourage the missionaries. God made sure His name was known, even in the jungles of Brazil. Even though everything went wrong at the beginning, God worked it out. We had trusted Him to provide for us and give us the strength and courage needed to finish the mission at hand. I had a wonderful experience in Brazil ministering to people and stepping out of my comfort zone. I had to depend on God as I had no idea what to expect. I was learning that taking a step of faith is believing that God will do the work. He is the one that is faithful.

3

Mentorship

A s Colleen and I continued our life together, I could see we thought about church differently. Colleen wanted to serve in ministry with me. She worked with youth but I just did not seem to catch that vision. I had no aspiration to be a pastor or leader. I perceived the church as a place to seek and worship God. I sensed that community was important but had no idea how important it is. I wanted to know God more, but my view of Him was limited; however, it was expanding.

During this time, the Scriptures started to become more important to me. I was fortunate enough to have a good mentor who showed me Jesus from cover to cover of the Bible. His counsel for interpreting the Scriptures was to keep Jesus in mind with the Bible from the Old Testament to New Testament. He showed me that God's character does not change, and He never makes a promise He cannot keep. God's character never changes as He is the same yesterday, today, and forever.

This mentor taught a Bible study from the Minor and Major Prophets of the Old Testament for approximately two years. The words *minor* and *major* did not refer to importance but rather reflected the volume of material written. It was a long class and I learned a lot. I realized how important prophets and prophecy are. A prophet is one who speaks for God to the people as God's mouthpiece. About one-quarter of the Bible is prophecy and most of it has come to fruition.

As I studied the prophets, especially Isaiah, I discovered that there were many prophecies about Jesus. In Isaiah chapter 53, the prophet Isaiah describes, in detail, Jesus's crucifixion that was well-documented nearly seven hundred years later in the four Gospels. Apart from the Bible, several other sources, found in the letters of Pliny the Younger to Emperor Trajan and writings from Josephus, indicate that Jesus was a real historical figure and was crucified. As there were many other prophecies in the Bible about Jesus's life that have come true, it validated the Bible as the Word of God. A mathematician calculated that a person predicting seven future events and getting them all right was the equivalent of marking one-quarter coin with an x on it and finding it by chance in quarters dropped two-feet deep in an area the size of Texas. I am certainly no mathematician but those odds are too mind-boggling to think about. Let alone there were many other prophecies about world events that have already come true.

Many of the prophets, as well as speaking about judgment, were also speaking of a literal savior who had the power to save from that very judgment. Also connecting the Old Testament to the New Testament is important as 10 percent of the Old Testament is repeated in the New Testament. For example, the words "It is written" or "To fulfill" in the New Testament are found 119 times. This study opened my eyes to how reliable and sacred the Scriptures are.

I always said my mentor was serious about the Bible. I later found out that the two-year course we studied was the short version. *WOW!* This guy was serious about the Bible. His intense passion for the Bible was contagious and he was a disciple-maker. He wanted to teach others who in turn could become disciples themselves. Thank God for people like him and others who were willing to disciple me.

I also developed a good relationship with a friend from St. John's Lutheran Church. We went through a men's retreat together. Colleen would later attend a women's retreat as well. This retreat showed the unconditional love of God and how it works in community. Up to this point, I had not experienced the kind of love that can be developed in community by being served by others. We ate all our meals together and did group activities. We sang together, worshipped, laughed, and cried together.

As the weekend progressed, I started to trust my community more and more. As a group we would also go to chapel to worship and praise God together. We would all listen to Rollos (teachings that promoted community, serving, giving, and loving one another). We would then break down into smaller groups to discuss the teachings and pray for one another. These smaller groups helped me build a sense of community that went way beyond just hanging out and getting to know one another.

The retreat weekend shifted from not only serving each other but how we could serve others once it was finished. Near the end of the weekend, it was revealed that the whole community experience had been bathed in prayer by others. Every hour around the clock, there were prayer partners who were praying for each individual candidate, each table, and the team. They also prayed about specific things that came up during the weekend. Just the thought of how much love and effort had been put into the weekend overwhelmed me. I finished the weekend strong and anticipated that God would continue the good work that He had started.

After completing the weekend retreat, I began meeting with my friend from the weekend. We would meet weekly at fast-food place and we talked about our successes and failures. We reminisced about our weekend and how the experience had impacted our lives. We were holding each other accountable to what we had learned and what new things we were learning. Both of us volunteered to be on teams for the retreat for many years afterward. It taught me a lot more about community and gave me a foretaste of the discipleship process.

As my confidence started to increase, I was asked to give what is called a Rollo (teaching) on one of the weekends. I had a hard time seeing myself as a teacher. I had a lot to learn but was willing to try. Over the next few years, my confidence continued to increase, and I was able to volunteer to give more Rollos.

As the years passed, my friend and I talked about how we could develop our relationship with Jesus better. We also discussed how we could utilize God's Word and our church community to improve our relationship with Him and serve others. My friend's wisdom and patience were incredible. I learned a lot about marriage, parenting, and life in general. He was a teacher with good awareness into how to help others solve problems. His insight helped me in seeing both sides of the coin. He would often say, "There are two sides to every story, but the truth usually lies somewhere near the middle."

Over the years we saw our kids grow up and become adults. We would share the changes and phases of life experiences over many years. We faithfully met almost every Saturday from 1994 to 2016. We were doing "life-on-life" discipleship. This is a crucial step in the discipleship process. I continued to be a learner in this process. I turned my failures into successes by learning and trying again. Over the years, I have had several other mentors who have spent a lot of time with me to develop my Christian walk and build my identity in Christ. God was building my character by using others to help me become more like Christ.

As I continued being mentored, I transitioned from my job working at the hospital to my next job at a local mental health agency. It seemed that I was building an unbelievable employment record even though I had failed at my first legitimate job. Again, I was truthful about my former experience of resigning and what had happened. Again, someone was willing to take a risk and hire me anyway. I immediately took the test to become a certified social worker for the state of Ohio. I passed the test after being hired as a case manager.

As a case manager, I had a smaller caseload of clients who had severe mental health diagnoses (many times, more than one). I served this population by educating them about mental health issues and becoming an advocate for them to navigate the different local and governmental systems. Many of these systems included medical treatment, social services, and community resources.

As a case manager, I never knew exactly what I was going to get into. I often monitored medication compliance and symptoms from the client's illness. I helped clients learn and manage daily living skills to improve their quality of life. I became a taxi service as transportation usually was an issue. I sometimes cleaned apartments and moved many a client after an eviction. Managing money was often a problem and the agency had to step in and become a representative payee. Helping clients find and maintain employment was a huge challenge. Much of what I did seemed to be damage control. Hence the words "case manager."

I helped clients to develop an individual service plan (ISP). This ISP would aid in developing treatment goals and potential outcomes. The ISP allowed the client and me to monitor their progress and address new goals as their situation changed. The ISP also helped to expand the options that were available and put more control in the hands of the client.

The overarching goal was to use outpatient therapies and community connections to assist clients in maintaining themselves in a community environment. Sometimes this strategy was not enough, and clients had to be hospitalized for their own safety and the safety of others. Many times, it was difficult to determine public safety issues over individual rights. At times, this public safety versus personal rights issue created a real challenge to figure out what was the ethical and responsible solution.

Even though there were difficult issues, I learned a lot about myself and others while working in the mental health field. I had bosses who were able to model behavior that encouraged me and pushed me to step out of my comfort zone to serve others.

They helped to mentor me in relating to others and how to be successful on the job. They were patient with me as I was too eager to learn. I am a task-oriented person and it took time to move toward relationships versus just completing the task. I was thankful to have had bosses, for the most part, who believed in me and saw that I was an extremely hard worker. They saw my potential, not my flaws. However, they did want me to work on my flaws so that I could more effectively reach, teach, and motivate others to see their potential.

As well, I had many colleagues that would encourage me and teach me along the way. My colleagues would see me at my best and at my worst. They did see that I had a sincere heart to help others and the patience to move others toward recovery.

I would work at the local mental health agency for ten years. I would develop relationships over those years with staff and clients that forever changed me. I was able to experience the highs and lows of humanity. Unfortunately, more lows than highs. Despite the lows, I rarely became discouraged. I had to keep things in perspective so that I could do my job and maintain my own mental health stability.

Many clients suffered from horrible abuse issues and addictions that often clouded their judgment in most areas of their lives. Some ended up in the legal system which confounded issues even more. Some were chronically mentally ill and there did not seem to be much hope that things would change. Some became so depressed or out of control that suicide seemed to be the only option.

Fortunately, mentors would be there for me during the good and the bad. They would assist me in learning how to take care of myself mentally and physically. These mentors would make sure that I did not take my work home with me.

When I finished a day's work, I went home to my family knowing I had done my best and that I could not change the world or solve all the problems of others. My work and family life were separate. I would not allow one to affect the other or vice versa. I did, however, feel a connection with those who were troubled and needed help. Somehow, I tended to connect with the down-and-out because I know how it feels to be down-and-out. Failing is not fun, but in the long run, it builds character if a person can learn from it and turn to God for repentance. I have always pulled for the underdog and consider myself one. Who does not like to root for the underdog?

4

Life in Jail

After ten years of working at the mental health agency, I changed directions and started working at a local jail in Newark, Ohio. Initially, it took so long to be hired that I almost gave up hope that it would work out. The hiring process took nearly six months, but I was finally hired under a four-year grant to work as a liaison of the Licking County Sheriff's Department to the probation department. My official title was "forensic social worker." In laymen's terms, it meant I was a case manager in a jail setting.

I would work with inmates who were released from jail and connect them to outside resources. One of these resources was the probation department. The probation officers helped to develop a plan that would ensure terms of the probation were maintained. The main population I served had serious mental health issues. This tended to complicate my work. Most of the clients had more than one issue to address and usually there were multiple issues that needed to be addressed.

Once released from jail the primary focus was trying to keep them out of jail. A lot of the clients were dealing with addiction issues. Many had made poor decisions and had little or no support outside the jail. These poor decisions caused countless family issues and problems. This resulted in many broken relationships, which generally filtered into every other aspect of their life. Poor follow-up on the client's part made tracking individuals and getting them to appointments quite difficult.

As well, some fell into their old patterns of criminal behavior. Many of the clients relapsed on alcohol or drugs. These patterns almost always resulted in them getting into further trouble. It also resulted in the client not going to the probation department and deviating from the original probation plan. In those cases, the writing was on the wall: back to jail they went. Now, in defense of the probation officers, I soon realized that most people were given several chances before their probation was revoked. Nevertheless, recidivism was and still is a major problem in the corrections system.

After four years in the jail under the original grant, my time ran out. The jail decided to keep me on, but my responsibilities changed. I transitioned to working inside the jail instead of outside. It was quite different working inside the jail. Things are much more controlled in a jail setting. I had become used to working outside the jail with less structure. The rules were quite different and there were a whole set of new obstacles to face.

Conflict or crisis management is one of the biggest problems in a jail setting. It seemed as if there was conflict at every turn—conflict with the other inmates, deputies, rules, judges, their family on the outside, the jail doctor, nursing staff, and even conflict with the social-work department.

Conflict abounded and seemed a way of life. Crisis situations were the norm, and most inmates did not handle these crisis situations well. Living in tight quarters often intensified negative reactions. I think most of what I did in the jail was put out fires. Not just small fires, but sometimes raging infernos. Thank God that when the fires were too big, I had backup. Again, my skills of presenting peace and patience seemed to extinguish many of those fires.

Contraband coming into the jail was also a big issue. Guarding against contraband coming into the jail was a constant priority as maintaining safety and security trumped almost all other issues. Being alert for such things is a priority and can make the difference between things running smoothly or having a disaster, which could put many in harm's way. Becoming complacent on this issue was not an option due to the nature of possible escape or injury to staff and other inmates.

Another problem that I noted was I felt like I was putting a bandage on a bleeding artery. The jail experience did not change a lot of people. Once released, many cleaned up their act for a short time. Many fell back in their old patterns. Their hearts were still the same. The jail experience was not necessarily changing behaviors. Some negatively dealt with their problems and issues for years. It was unrealistic that they could change overnight. Upon leaving the jail, changes were usually temporary, and a fair percentage went back to jail for a probation violation or a new charge.

Going to jail for many creates anxiety and shame. Being locked up creates stress that causes a flight-or-fight syndrome. Being in jail, you can do neither. Many must find a new way to adapt. While in jail, inmates often appear to be very needy. I guess you would be needy too, if you lost everything (including your freedom). It is called the domino effect. When a person goes to jail, they lose their freedom, sometimes their job, and usually a lot more. The losses are tremendous.

Sometimes the losses are so great that some lose hope completely and suicide seems to be the only way out. I remember three people committing suicide in a one-year stretch. The staff walked on pins and needles during that year. It was probably the most difficult year for me as well. Many of the changes that were made during that time would have ramifications for many years to come regarding the implementation of suicide protocol. Suicide prevention measures would never be 100-percent perfect, but it was unquestionably critical for the safety and maintenance of the jail population.

I worked at the jail for fifteen years and there were a total of eight suicides. There were so many suicide attempts that it would be hard to come up with an actual number of them. Most attempts were a cry for help or an attempt to control the situation, but a few were bent on complete destruction. Hopelessness drives people to do the unimaginable.

Depression and anxiety go hand in hand with the jail experience. Sometimes it was difficult to determine true mental health issues from depression and anxiety related to the jail experience itself. Depression in jail is an ongoing issue that fluctuated with changes within the module/cell block, court dates, outside family issues, sentencing, and just the boredom of being in jail. Some inmates began to look to God because of their profound depression and hopelessness.

Fortunately, the jail had a chaplain who was good at connecting with others and meeting their spiritual needs. He had a story that could give hope. He once lived on the other side of the tracks, but Christ intervened in his life and gave him hope. One time, I called on the jail chaplain when an inmate was suicidal after getting the news he would be going to prison. This inmate was able to connect with him (the jail chaplain) immediately. The chaplain had been in serious legal trouble yet somehow God had used him. So much so he had become a minister. The jail chaplain shared his story of hope and it made all the difference for that inmate and many others. After the chaplain talked with the inmate, he had enough courage to face the unpleasantness of prison. He had hope that not all was lost.

I often referred inmates to the jail chaplain for counseling or if they had spiritual questions. Many wanted a Bible or to be baptized. In the last few years, an average of 225 inmates have made decisions to be saved by Jesus. One hundred ten inmates were baptized, and 842 Bibles were handed out. Many had questions about faith due to their difficult circumstances.

The jail chaplain had a connection with the local ministerial association. Many of those of the local ministerial association would lead Bible studies and mentor inmates while in jail. The chaplain also had a program called "Be a Friend." These friends were mentors who helped support inmates while in jail as well as connecting with them on the outside. Even so, it was rough sailing for many who became entangled in the corrections system. Many did not develop a safety network in or out of the jail. Many of those continued to come back to jail.

The whole jail experience is based on punishment. I understand the whole punishment concept. I am in total agreement that a person should be responsible for his/her own behavior. If a law is broken there needs to be a consequence. One of the issues is that when consequences are strictly based on fear, there is a problem. Punishment that is strictly based on fear is usually not a deterrent for people to change their behavior. How do I know that? Check the recidivism rate. The current rate for being rearrested in the US within three years of release is about two-thirds. Within five years of release about three-quarters of released prisoners were rearrested. What is the answer? Perfect love casts out fear.

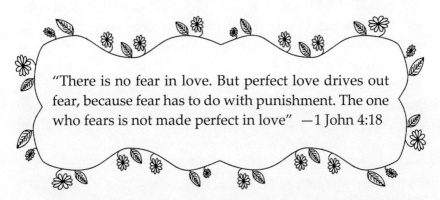

"There is no fear in love. But perfect love drives out fear, because fear has to do with punishment. The one who fears is not made perfect in love" —1 John 4:18

What is perfect love? God sent His Son Jesus to take the punishment that our sin deserved. That is perfect love. Again, it is a heart issue. I was not always sure what my role was with sharing my faith at the jail. When inmates were willing to discuss faith issues, I was more than willing to go there. Otherwise, there seemed to be a lot of questions. I did know that changing the system was not something I could do. I saw so many people over the years try to change others or something that was not in their control. This led to frustration and, many times, even anger. I did know that God called me to be fair and honest with people. God wanted me to show compassion but also wanted me to teach how to live a controlled life within the confines of the jail's rules/regulations. He wanted me to be faithful. These things I could do with God's help.

My attention sometimes spilled over to the staff who had to deal with many of the mental health issues they saw at work as well as issues of their own. Stress can take its toll on anyone. Prolonged stress can cause physical and emotional issues. Responding quickly is important. Being a good listener is also crucial in helping others. Being able to restate exactly what is said is of utmost importance. This helps with the process of understanding one another. It also develops trust. One rule that is important with trust is to never promise something that you cannot deliver on. Treating everyone fairly and with dignity also builds trust.

Over the years, I had seen and helped a lot of inmates and staff to shift their thinking so that they could at least see the light at the end of the tunnel. Giving people options rather than telling them what to do empowered them to make better decisions. Even so, many would be facing issues that they would struggle with and not be able to see that light. Over the years at the jail, I often sensed that my efforts fell short of giving true hope. I did feel that God was using me, but I sensed I could do more. I wondered about this and, for some reason, could not see myself retiring at the jail.

Despite the complicated issues, I liked working at the jail. I considered my unique position and the progress that some made. I wanted to help others and see my community improve and thrive. It was important to help others to reach their true potential so that all of society benefits. It was important to express and show my faith but to do it in a way that honored God and people. I guess this was the issue I struggled with the most. How do I minister to people in jail within the context of my Christian faith and walk?

I guess this question forced me to think about the bigger picture and what my role was. I was happy and satisfied with the job overall, but I often felt God had something bigger for me. Many times, I prayed that He would reveal that "something else" to me. It took a long time for this prayer to be answered, but God was faithful. He always is. However, if God answered all my prayers immediately, I would have little or no chance to develop deep character traits that result from perseverance. That is the bigger picture. God's overall character is what is important. It is important how His character influences us. I knew that God would not and could not abandon me.

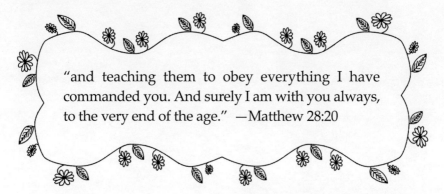

"and teaching them to obey everything I have commanded you. And surely I am with you always, to the very end of the age." —Matthew 28:20

I knew God would be faithful to help me through this life journey, no matter what might happen. This was instilled in me after accepting Christ as my Savior and only grew in intensity as I continued my Christian walk by faith.

5

Winds of Change

In 2008, Colleen planned a surprise trip to the Grand Canyon. I always wanted to go to the Grand Canyon. I liked the Wild Wild West. I had been drawn to the West several times, visiting South Dakota and Wyoming. I enjoyed the history of the Old West and the majesty and splendor of the mountains. I enjoyed visiting national treasures and seeing God's wonderful creation. Before leaving to see the Grand Canyon, I prayed to God to show me more than just the Grand Canyon. As my brother would say, "It's just a big hole in the ground." I wanted something meaningful. I wanted God to reveal Himself, and boy did He ever deliver.

Before leaving, our pastor from our local Alive Vineyard Church asked us to look up a small Vineyard church in Flagstaff, Arizona. We decided to visit that church on a Sunday morning before heading up to the canyon. I remember approaching the building and thinking, *This cannot be a church*. It certainly did not look like a typical church. That day, this small church was holding a service about missionaries and giving testimonies about persecution around the world.

At the time, I was unaware of a special day called the International Day of Prayer for the Persecuted Church. It was the only day out of the year when such a service was held, and it was not a coincidence that we were there. This church remembered those who had sacrificed so much for the Gospel. It was quite different from any other church service I had ever attended. The service was extremely basic. No frills and no thrills. There were no seats, so we had to sit on the floor. There was no air conditioning, the lighting was low, you had to be quiet, and no excessive celebrating was allowed. Comfort was not high on the list of priorities.

There was a lot of prayer and I heard stories from missionaries telling how God was working in other countries. It was not long before I started to sense that I had become quite complacent and comfortable. "Church" was being held without all the bells and whistles. What a novel thought. Worshipping and praising God without getting bogged down with all the extras. It was a refreshing way to help the congregation stay focused on God and what He was doing in the world.

As the service progressed, it took a turn that completely caught me off guard. The missionaries started showing pictures of Christians from around the world who had been persecuted for their faith, some for having a Bible or praying. They showed picture after picture of those who had lost so much. However, there seemed to be a contentment in their eyes and faces. Some had lost their whole family, yet there was a peace about them. I had a hard time understanding why they were smiling and seemed so joyful. How could they have peace? How could they have joy? Their joy certainly was not about their circumstances.

I was having trouble wrapping my mind around the service and became overwhelmed. Then, as if to build a crescendo, I saw pictures of men and women who had been in jail for having a Bible, sharing their faith, or worshipping God. It started with only a few days in jail. Picture after picture showed an increase in the amount of jail time. The weight of their suffering started to cause me inward turmoil. Soon, the number of days in jail had built up to 3,500 days. All for the name of Christ. It broke my heart.

I cried until I could not cry anymore. I felt utter despair. Their pain became my pain and it seemed relentless. Physical pain is one thing. Taking the pain of another is taking pain to a new level. Even as I am writing this, my eyes start to well up. It was one of those powerful experiences that was etched in my mind forever.

It seemed that God was leading us in the right direction toward a next step. God broke my heart for my fellow Christians who were persecuted for Christ's name.

From that moment, I sensed that God had a plan for my life. The truth was He always had a plan for me, I just was not always able to see it. I had no idea what the plan looked like or how it would work out. I had a lot of questions, but I was confident that God would be with me all the way and that He would be the differencemaker.

After visiting that small church, we headed north to see the Grand Canyon. The view was much more spectacular than I could have ever imagined.

Pictures do not do it justice. However, the view was pale in significance when compared to how God had touched my heart in Flagstaff. I was confident that God would do something amazing and open the door to launch us forward.

After seeing the Grand Canyon and finishing our vacation, we returned to Ohio. Shortly after arriving, the coordinators of our local church's mission team stepped down. The church leadership and others asked me if I would be interested in the position. I am not a rocket scientist, so this seemed like a no-brainer. After my experience in Flagstaff, Arizona, it certainly seemed to be the thing to do. I remembered my prayer before visiting the canyon. I did not want to hastily decide based on subjective feelings.

After consideration with prayer, Colleen and I decided to take on the task of leading our church's mission team. We took it over with great enthusiasm and joy, hoping and praying as God opened the door for us. Our church in general was a very mission-minded church so this helped with the transition. Also, the mission team was incredibly supportive of us right from the beginning. Leading was probably not our forte but we knew that we needed to step into that role by faith. This was all new to us, but we believed God would give us what we needed to do the job.

As we began to meet and get to know each other, we started looking in more detail about the specific missions our team supported financially. Even though I was a member of the Alive Vineyard Church, I was unaware of the different missions that our church supported locally and abroad. I wondered about the disconnect. I kept this in mind as we moved forward.

We had several meetings and I soon discovered that there was a budget to meet and much of our time was spent working on that end of things. Not being financially savvy, it soon turned into a struggle. Unfortunately, finances were not our cup of tea. I was thinking relationship-versus-budget needs. I continued to think about my own disconnect with the various missions supported.

Undaunted, I decided to have each team member pick a mission that our church supported financially. Then each team member could start building a relationship with that mission. After building a relationship, each person would report back to the team what was happening. As a result, our team could develop a more specific plan and prayer strategy for each of the missions supported financially. I also thought it would encourage us as a team to hear testimonies of God's work that we were investing in.

There was some success, but the finances still seemed to bog me down. I had many conversations with God; this was not what I had signed up for. I was somewhat confused and wondered where God was going with all this. Again, I felt frustrated but was resolute. I was determined to start thinking outside the box.

I often thought of the overseas missionaries whom our church supported. I wondered about them and how they were making an impact for Christ. I decided that someone should try to visit our overseas missionaries. That "someone" became Colleen and me. We looked at the overseas missions our church supported and soon became interested in Macedonia.

Our church supported missionaries who were ministering in Macedonia with Campus Crusade for Christ (CCC, now CRU). They had been in Macedonia for about six years and had started working with college students at the main university in the capital city of Skopje. CCC staff were developing a network of contacts and were mentoring many students. Those who responded to the

Gospel were being mentored on how to live out their faith and share it with others. I wanted to see how things worked firsthand. I am a hands-on guy, so I liked the idea of learning the "nuts and bolts" of how a missionary lived. I wondered what the missionaries did on a day-to-day basis to make a difference in other people's lives. I wanted to know how they were sharing Christ and what was their vision for Macedonia.

In 2011, we started making plans to begin fundraising to go to Macedonia for their summer project called "Speak Out." Speak Out was based on faith that comes from hearing the Word of God. Hearing the story of salvation through a testimony or the Gospel about Jesus. Our local Vineyard church supported us by helping with several fundraisers. We were able to get the funds needed to go and this greatly increased our faith in God; it greatly increased our trust in God and his ability to provide for us.

We purchased our tickets and we anticipated that God was going to move in a mighty way. We were now moving from just influencing our Jerusalem to possibly influencing Samaria and beyond. Maybe around the world. We were extremely excited about the prospects as three years had elapsed since starting as mission team coordinators. Things seemed to be moving at a snail's pace, but some of the pieces were coming together to launch us into a cross-cultural experience. This experience would lay the groundwork for further involvement in the mission field.

As we were planning details to travel to Macedonia, I began to develop some health problems. I experienced severe leg spasms that incapacitated me. One night I fell out of bed with spasms in my calf. As I lay on the floor, my other calf did the same thing. I could not get off the floor. Colleen called to wake up our children in desperation. All of them helped me off the floor. I felt very weak and humbled. At the time it was scary, but afterward, we all had a good laugh. However, something was obviously wrong, and I needed answers.

I had several tests done. An MRI showed that at some point in my life I had broken my back. Earlier in my life, I had broken my femur and often wondered if the two might be related. At that time, I spent twelve weeks fully incapacitated unable to get out of bed. It took nearly a year to learn to walk without a limp. I had a hard time understanding how I could have broken my back without knowing it. There were other surgeries in the past that may have contributed to the problem. I also completed a test to check the firing of neurons in my legs. My legs were so tight, I could hardly stand it. There did not seem to be an answer from the past that would correct the current problem.

When the results came back from all the tests, I had seven different diagnoses on my back. The official decision was that I needed back surgery. I needed a steel rod to keep my spine from completely falling apart. *No way*, I thought. *I am going to Macedonia in a few weeks.* I wanted a second opinion. The second opinion was that my back was completely shot–official diagnosis. I decided to schedule the surgery after my return from Macedonia. Not a good call.

One night as I was writhing in pain, I got up and looked in the mirror. I cried out to God, "I can't do this. I need to cancel going to Macedonia." A calmness came over me like nothing I had ever experienced before. It was as if God was saying, "Go and I'll be with you. It will be okay." What happened next absolutely perplexed me. It shook me to the core. I soon had a sense that things would get much worse. That, I did not want to hear. Things were bad enough so I could not conceive of things getting worse. Again, a peace came over me reassuring me that I should go to Macedonia. I sensed that God would work things out. I surrendered to the idea that only He could work it out.

In my heart, I knew that I was so weak and broken physically that there was no other choice but to trust Him. Not only that, but I would be doing His work. He convinced me with His calmness and goodness that He would not forsake or leave me. As I continued to ponder this thought, I put my faith and trust in Him that He would be faithful to see me through this.

Many of my friends, both Christians and non-Christians, tried to persuade me not to go.

"Look at all your health problems."

"What if something goes wrong while you're in Macedonia and you end up in the hospital?"

"It's a very unwise decision to go."

I heard it all. Somehow, God instilled in me a rock-solid faith that He would deliver as promised. My job was to be faithful and not complain, not to be fearful, not to let others influence me when I had clearly heard that it would be okay.

Through the increased pain, sweating, tiredness, and lethargy, God gave me a calmness that could only come from Him. I hung onto that as if it were my security blanket. I just had an over-whelming sense that God would be faithful no matter what obstacles I would face. It is weird because things did get worse. I am talking much worse. However, I had a joy that cannot be explained. Even though this was not direct persecution, I started to understand how the Christians from my Flagstaff experience could have joy despite tremendous pain and adversity. I started to discover that, despite circumstances, I could still be joyful. My faith was in the Lord and His great character. I was thankful and continued to pray a lot. God was faithful to hear my prayers.

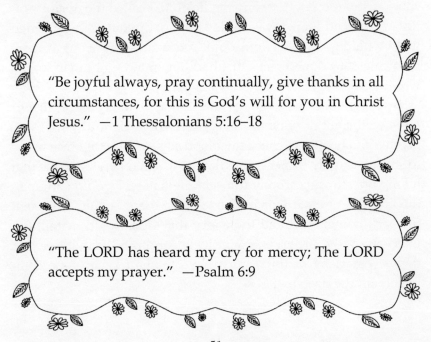

"Be joyful always, pray continually, give thanks in all circumstances, for this is God's will for you in Christ Jesus." —1 Thessalonians 5:16–18

"The LORD has heard my cry for mercy; The LORD accepts my prayer." —Psalm 6:9

When I got worse, I was not worried. God had this one.

I continued to move forward. I planned to leave on a Saturday for Macedonia. I had finished all my pre-surgery tests and had planned to have the back surgery after returning from Macedonia. I received a call at work on Friday morning. It was the doctor's office. They canceled my surgery due to an elevated blood sugar level of nearly four hundred. I needed to be on medication immediately. The medication would be called into the local pharmacy. Again, the advice was not good. The doctor wanted me to cancel my trip.

Later in the day after work, I stopped at the pharmacy to pick up my medication. To my surprise, the pharmacist could not find that any medication had been ordered. I explained the gravity of the situation. The pharmacist called the doctor's office several times with no response. The pharmacist also left several messages. It was too late in the day to go to the doctor's office as they would be closed before I arrived. The pharmacist requested I come back tomorrow morning. He was confident (and so was I) that considering the circumstances, I would get the medication I needed.

I arrived when the pharmacy opened the next day. To my shock, I still did not have any medication. I called the doctor's office again to no avail. I was baffled but not discouraged. I decided that I would go to Macedonia and God would figure out the rest, medicines or no medicines. If I had depended on human logic I would have folded. I would have given up.

By faith, I decided to go to Macedonia. That day at the airport there were a lot of prayers and concerns, and rightfully so. I was given a glucometer to check my blood sugar. I was told by a nurse to stop all carbohydrates immediately. It was reiterated to me that if I did not stop all carbohydrates immediately, I would end up in the hospital or even worse. The "even worse" should have sent me back home, but I had to believe that God would be faithful. Everyone at the airport was genuinely concerned. I could see it in their eyes. Many of them must have thought I had gone completely off the deep end.

Colleen and I departed for Macedonia and trusted that God would be faithful. The flight was uneventful, and I did not experience any problems physically. I stopped all carbohydrates immediately. Talk about going through withdrawal. I love to eat bread, pasta, and sweets, all the wrong things for a person with my condition. However, after three days, I discovered that it became easier to keep the no-carb diet. My craving for carbohydrates diminished considerably. Also, a missionary from CCC made an appointment for me to see an Indian doctor. The doctor gave me some herbs and vitamins to take. I still needed to continue with the no-carbohydrate diet. Boo-hoo!

While I was in Macedonia, I started to become stronger, and each day my blood sugar began to drop. Thank God for the glucometer. However, I was not out of the woods yet. One night I was lying in bed and became paralyzed. I could not even call or move to reach out to Colleen, who was sleeping right beside me. It was the strangest feeling. Fortunately, before retiring to bed I had put my headphones on to listen to some Christian music. I prayed a lot as that seemed to be all I could do. I closed my eyes and hoped I would not die. I continued to pray a lot. I thought, somehow, I would find enough strength to wake Colleen so I could go to the hospital. The music helped my mind to finally relax and I soon fell asleep.

In the morning, I rolled over and I wondered if I had been dreaming. Trust me, that was no dream. Pain like that does not exist in a dream. However, I felt renewed and was confident that it would be okay. God had my back literally and figuratively. I was, in fact, still alive. As Colleen woke up from her sleep, she asked me if everything was okay. I simply said, "Now that I'm awake, I'm good." That certainly had not been the case the night before.

With renewed strength, I pushed forward. I knew that there was an outreach planned that day and I was not going to miss it. We went to the beach and met with many Macedonians, mainly youth. I listened as CCC staff members shared their faith and testimonies. I felt helpless sharing because of the language barrier so

I prayed a lot. Even with the language barrier, it became evident that people wanted to know why Colleen and I came all the way from "little old" Newark, Ohio, to visit Macedonia.

I remember giving a man a Bible translated into Macedonian. He began weeping. It was very touching. What I did not realize was in Macedonia no one gives anything without expecting something in return. There is always a catch. The fact that I gave him something unconditionally brought him to tears. I hoped that he would read the word and somehow find his way to God. I also gave some baseball caps away with Christian logos on them. The same thing happened. Macedonians found it hard to believe that someone would give freely without expecting something in return.

Colleen and staff from CCC encountered people at the beach, on the streets, and in their homes. A national missionary took Colleen to visit homes around the neighborhood. They saw a *baba* (grandmother) working in her garden. She reminded Colleen of her grandma who came from Serbia. They introduced themselves and she invited them into her home. Other team members showed up. Baba gave the group a snack and started talking with one of the team leaders. As they left, Colleen learned that when someone offers food or drink, you accept it without hesitation. Being hospitable was a way that Macedonians showed their love and appreciation. To reject such hospitality would be disrespectful and dishonorable.

Colleen and the team also went to the beach and it was Colleen's time to share. She had trouble expressing herself. As a large crowd formed around all of them, she became extremely nervous. When she was finished, her prayer was that the Lord would use what she had said for His glory. He would be faithful and fix what was said or not said.

Colleen also met three Muslim teenagers. Her team shared the Gospel with them, but they were not interested. The teen girls were wearing bikinis, and this surprised Colleen. The team questioned the teens about this since this type of behavior was not seen as acceptable in their culture. The teens responded, "Our fathers are not around, so we can do whatever we want." While the cat's away, the mice will play.

We saw that there were many in Macedonia who professed faith but had no idea what that meant. They knew a few phrases or buzzwords but could not express anything else about their faith. They believed that people were born Christian or Muslim because of where they were born. They were born into a religion. They were cultural Muslim believers.

One of the reasons we went to Macedonia was to attend a summer project called Speak Out. This was the first summer project planned by CCC. Even the staff from CCC were not quite sure how it would work out. There did not seem to be a definite strategy at the time.

Much of what we did was simply share and pray with others. I enjoyed talking with the Macedonians and getting to know the culture. I had always seen "culture" as a negative word. It seemed somewhat nationalistic and seemed to separate people who think and act differently; little did I know. I came to appreciate culture in a new way that unlocked something in me. I enjoyed my time with the CCC staff by getting to know and encouraging them. I discovered that missionaries often lead lonely lives on the mission field and need encouragement. They need contact from others outside their circle of personal influence who can support and encourage them.

Encouragement can come in many forms. Colleen also needed encouragement. She felt exhausted and even walking seemed to be a chore. She avoided talking about her feelings. She was having bad dreams. She began to wonder if Satan was attacking her. She soon began to sense that the attacks were indeed spiritual in nature. Her health was starting to fail as well. Through all that, Colleen remained faithful and available. She was seeing God work and that encouraged her greatly. She was not quite sure how things were going to work out, but she could see God being faithful.

As part of our preparation for Speak Out we were required to read the book by John Ortberg, *If You Want to Walk on Water,*

You've Got to Get Out of the Boat, and give a talk to the students who attended the Speak Out. Colleen and I did not have a chance to read the book, so we listened to it on tape as we were traveling to Lake Ohrid in the south of Macedonia. Colleen thought, "WOW!" She needed to think about this and how she was going to report about it. The phrase "getting out of the boat" resonated with me. I had never looked at it that way. I simply saw the walking on water. It is a risk to even get out of the boat in the first place. It takes effort to even entertain the idea that one could walk on water.

Each of us worked on a report of what we learned from the book and how it applied to what we were currently doing. Colleen and I had split our talks. The interesting thing was that we had not been given a chance to speak with each other beforehand. God simply confirmed this message without us consulting one another. I cannot remember all the specifics about what was said. I do remember that it took us back to Abraham and how he was faithful to "step out of the boat" and take a risk by going to a foreign land. God showed us exactly what to say.

Taking the risk to go was simply the beginning. It was the first step on a much longer journey.

As time went on, I became physically stronger. I was able to run up a hill to go to a monastery for prayer. Some of the staff started to wonder whether there was anything wrong with me. Colleen seemed to gain confidence as well. Many of her problems began to subside. God was doing something utterly amazing. It was truly a transformation.

Our trip was not over yet. We went to Greece and saw many of the historical relics in Philippi that had survived several large earthquakes. The area had been completely abandoned between the fourteenth and fifteenth centuries. We received a good history lesson. We saw the dungeon where Paul had been imprisoned. The architecture of the basilica was incredible. We walked the Roman Road, visited the amphitheater where the Romans had killed Christians, and we swam and waded in the river where Lydia had been baptized. It was truly astonishing to see such things and places that were straight from biblical times. It was all so surreal.

Next, we went to Bradford, England, where we stayed with another missionary. In Bradford, I was exposed to a different way of life than in Macedonia or the US. We were only there for a few days, but it was the relationships that seemed to catch my attention more than ever. This missionary enjoyed meeting with and ministering to Muslims. As we were visiting Bradford, I discovered that one of the biggest mosques west of Istanbul had been built shortly before our arrival. It was amazing to think about. How did that happen? There were no easy answers.

In Bradford, we were able to go downtown and set up a banner that said, "Pray for Bradford." It was incredible to simply pray for people.

Colleen looked for opportunities to pray. God sent an elderly lady her way. Colleen asked her if she needed prayer. The elderly lady said no very quickly. She then said, "God is dead and I don't believe in prayer." Somewhat surprised, Colleen quickly replied, "He is alive and loves you very much." The elderly lady started to ask Colleen why she was in Bradford and what sites she planned to see. The elderly lady insisted Colleen go to the abbey. This surprised Colleen even more as the older lady had just said there is no God. Before the elderly lady left, Colleen asked to pray for her again. The woman accepted Colleen's prayer for her and for her son who was sick. Amazing for a woman who had just said that God was dead and that she did not believe in prayer. Another seed was planted.

We really felt that God was moving. The ground that we prayed on was Holy ground; it was consecrated, set apart for prayer each week like clockwork. This missionary and others had been meeting every week for quite some time, ministering to the people of Bradford with prayer.

This missionary had worked in Bradford for years, specifically ministering to Muslims. He gave us a glimpse of reality that opened our eyes. He indicated that God was working among Muslims and others to reach people with the Gospel by giving them dreams and visions. Some of the Muslims were ending up in the United States. These dreams and visions were often related to Jesus. This missionary told us that our responsibility was to tell them that these dreams were indeed about Jesus. These dreams and visions were meant to lead them to Jesus. To me, this is a testament of God speaking to people directly, to reach them in a unique way. God was sending people to Europe, the United States, and other places because access to the Gospel was being cut off in hard-to-reach areas. Also, Christians had failed to go or could not go.

What I later learned was that many people were living in what is called the 10/40 window (a rectangular area of North Africa, the Middle East, and Asia, approximately between ten degrees and forty degrees latitude north of the equator)—an area of the globe that is difficult to gain access with the Gospel. However, God was getting around man's feeble attempt to shut Him out. He was making His name known to all cultures. He was also going to do this even though Christians refused to go or could not go.

I could see that God was doing something incredibly special. God helped us to understand that building relationships and community was vital in accomplishing His mission. God was exposing us to different cultures to show us that His heart was to reach all people despite their efforts to push Him away. I now began to see culture as okay. It was not a "negative" word anymore. It was different, but that was okay. As I began to travel around the world, I soon started to see things in my own culture that made me wonder.

When I returned from mission trips, I often felt reverse culture shock. There are so many options in the US, far more than most countries. I also recognized that our lifestyle is so hectic that we rarely have time to stop and smell the roses. In general, we seem to be less connected within a community context. People in many foreign countries do not live the way westerners do. Culture is what makes us different. Besides, God is the One who created culture. It is okay to be different, to be unique. However, if my intention is to reach the nations, then I must see things in a different way. I need to see things the way other people see them and put the Gospel into a context that can be understood. Truth is truth but relating it in a way that honors people and God will speak volumes about His love.

We returned to the States armed with a new and fresh look at culture. It was an eye-opener, to say the least. Some things had changed, but my spine was not one of them. Nearly a year later, I finally had the surgery that should have stopped me from going to Macedonia. During this process, I also discovered my upper back was damaged. More good news. Official diagnosis again.

The doctor offered to fuse my lower and upper back at the same time. I had no intention of walking around like Frankenstein. I was determined to have the doctor work on the worst part of my back and then take my chances with the rest.

After the surgery on my lower back, I developed a blood clot in my leg. I could have given up all hope. There were times when I felt like giving up, but I refused to do so, mainly because I knew God had a plan for me. I knew that He would always be faithful.

After four months, I finally recovered, and my diabetes seemed to be under control even without medications. The blood clot went away. However, I still had headaches. I had them for several years. I discovered that they were related to high blood pressure. Shortly after that, I developed high cholesterol and my diabetic issues came back. I was falling apart. I had other arthritis issues due to several injuries and surgeries.

My family doctor thought that I might have rheumatoid arthritis. I was referred to a specialist and further testing revealed that I had diffused idiopathic skeletal hyperostosis (DISH). It is an ugly disease (with an ugly name) that calcifies both ligaments and bones at an accelerated rate. There is no cure and it is a chronic progressive disease.

At the doctor's office, my orthopedic back specialist put his hand on Colleen's shoulder and said, "Please don't let your husband bend or twist abruptly." I guess he did not know me very well.

6

The Challenge

I n 2013, my life took a change in a new direction, a fresh direction. What happened would strengthen me, encourage me, and deepen my walk with the Lord even more than ever.

Colleen and I attended a mission's conference in Louisville, Kentucky, called Kairos, not to be confused with the prison ministry Kairos. It was a weeklong training in basic biblical foundations for missions. We went with a couple from our church. We all learned a lot, had fun, and laughed a lot. The conference started with the Abrahamic Covenant.

The conference showed us how being on mission with God can be a start to reaching the nations. There was a lot of reading and practical teachings that made me start to think about what missions might look like. I saw that God has always been on a mission from the creation of the world (and even before that). He was a missional God and wanted to restore humanity to Himself. The idea that we were created to glorify Him and Him alone was not new to us. We were also created to bless others because we have been blessed through Christ. During this conference, the idea came to my mind that I might quit my job and somehow end up on the mission field. That was a particularly strange thought, but intriguing nonetheless.

We went back to Ohio with an enhanced understanding of missions. I wanted to understand and know more before I proceeded forward. I had already figured out that God does not reveal all the details of His plan for us. There is an element of faith. Something did spark my curiosity about quitting my job.

Later in the year, I started to think more and more about my job. I resisted this thought at first, quitting my job seemed to be a radical idea. Besides, I needed a plan. I needed backup. I was comfortable and had my family to consider. I wondered about quitting my job and where it might take me. At the time, I was only looking at the things I would have to give up. I recalled the thoughts about wanting something different, the thoughts that God had something bigger and better for me. It became apparent to me that I could and would gain so much more if I stepped forward by faith.

As the intensity level about quitting my job increased, I began to see that God wanted me to drop everything and totally rely on Him. Again, I knew His promises about provision, His uniqueness, His trustworthiness, and His unchanging character. I knew that He would not abandon me. I felt an uneasiness about not accepting this challenge. I soon became overwhelmed by the need to obey and felt compelled to move forward in faith. I did not have a plan or any idea where this would take me. Steps of faith are often like that.

I was confident that God was behind me and would provide every step of the way. I knew God would be faithful to give me all the resources necessary to complete a job that He had given me. I considered all the things I had been given in my life. God had been so gracious to supply all my needs even though, many times, I had not asked Him for direction. I wanted to hear His voice and to be about my Father's business, not my own. I asked and it became very apparent what I needed to do. I needed to be faithful, available, and teachable. It was as if God was saying trust in Him and He will open the floodgates of heaven. Trust in Him and He will provide for me.

My mind flashed back to the book we read in Macedonia about getting out of the boat. There were many questions, but there only seemed to be one answer. I wanted to live a life of abundance because of His great overflow of love. I wanted more out of life and was convinced God wanted more for me too.

I mentioned my plans to others. Again, it did not go over well and was met with a great deal of resistance and skepticism. Many questioned whether I had heard from God. In my mind, I went back to my decision to go to Macedonia. In the world's eyes and even to some Christians, it seemed foolhardy. As critical as other people were, it forced me to look at what would happen if I did trust Him; what would be gained versus what would be lost was not the question to ask. It was all His anyway.

I knew that regarding my previous employment and other earlier considerations, I had not always consulted the Father. I began to understand that God was not interested in my skill set, my inclinations, or how religious I am. He simply wants me to worship Him alone and no one else, and to find out what His heart is. Then my response should be simply to obey.

I began to pour my heart out to God. My plea was to make sure that I heard Him correctly, and if so, it was "game on." As I prayed, a new sense of purpose came over me. Life did not seem to be about me anymore but only pleasing the One who created me. As I trusted God more, the Scriptures started to come to life again. As I sat in Sunday school each week, something was said or shown to me that confirmed what I was about to do.

I discussed with Colleen about my resignation. She had been preparing herself for this as well but in a different way. She had not planned on me resigning quite so quickly. She was thinking more about the planning stage. I threw caution to the wind and went into the office with my resignation in hand.

I gave the sheriff's department a two-month notice. I remember the sheriff coming into my office; he seemed perplexed. He asked me if I had any problems with the staff, inmates, or even at home. I thought that I had articulated in my letter why I was resigning. I guess not. It had nothing to do with my job satisfaction. I felt a calling for my life other than working at the jail. I expressed that there were no issues with personnel, inmates, or at home. I expressed my deepest satisfaction with the fact that I had worked at the jail for thirteen years and was grateful for what I had learned and experienced. It was a decision based on faith that God had a different purpose for my life. My circumstances now seemed temporary. I needed to put my trust in Him completely. Over the years, I had put my faith in the American Dream ("the American scheme"). Getting comfortable and planning for retirement should not be the goal. God was taking me out of my comfort zone, but I could see it was for my own good. I was ready to move forward instead of feeling stuck.

My immediate boss did not react well either. He was overwhelmed. I had tried to prepare him over the years for the day when I would step down as a social worker. I guess he did not believe me either. I told him that no one is indispensable and that the jail would be fine without me. I mentioned that he might be surprised to find out that someone more capable than me might just fill my position. My boss was not buying it. In fact, deep down, I felt a sadness.

Over the years I had developed a close relationship with my boss and would deeply miss him and others at the jail. My boss had trusted me to do the right thing in a timely manner. He had confidence in me that the job would get done. Again, I noted my gratefulness and appreciation for the opportunity to work at the jail. By working at the jail, I saw a different view of humanity that many people do not get a chance to see. Behavior is important, but it is not the whole story; it was people's heart condition that separated them from God. Jesus came to restore humanity's heart and to reconcile a broken relationship with the Father. God's great love is relentless in this endeavor.

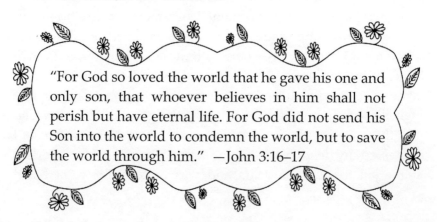

"For God so loved the world that he gave his one and only son, that whoever believes in him shall not perish but have eternal life. For God did not send his Son into the world to condemn the world, but to save the world through him." —John 3:16–17

This is the message I wanted to proclaim to all. God genuinely wanted to reach all the nations and I wanted to be a part of that. It became apparent to me that a lot of people were either stuck in the past or worried about the future; I wanted to live for the moment doing what the Father asked of me.

Resigning from the jail was a big step. I had no job, no plan, and no health insurance. What happened next was amazing. Within one month of resigning, the jail offered me to contract out with them and work eight hours a week. The jail offered to double my previous hourly wage. I would not have any benefits, but that seemed okay. I could also set my own hours each week. One other benefit was that I would only need to do the short mental health assessment, which the jail required on all inmates who would be there fourteen days or more. No more putting out fires. Hallelujah! Praise the Lord!

I prayed about this and accepted their offer. I would do this for another two years while planning out what ministry would look like and how to develop support. Shortly after that, I was able to secure another part-time job at a wood shop. That was much harder work physically, but it provided additional income.

The Lord had blessed me right away, and He was just getting started. This helped encourage me so much. God instilled in me that He would provide no matter what. My part was to be obedient to His calling. It was such a blessing to have two jobs and still consider options that allowed me to pursue the things of God. All I needed to do was to follow His lead and there would be much more to come. "I will never abandon you" meant more to me than ever before. God's unchangeable character was something I could completely trust in.

God was willing to immediately connect me with a missionary who would mentor me on my journey to be on mission with God. He was able to give me some sound advice. I needed it as this was all completely new to me. As all this unfolded, he was spot-on about most things.

At the time, I had no plan but knew I needed to step forward by faith. He did admit that he had never seen anyone start in missions the way I was doing it. He proposed that missionaries develop a sense of some type of plan and fill in the details as they go along. He advised me to start praying about an area in the world and/or a people group. I think he was a little bit skeptical, but he wanted to pray for me. He also wanted me to keep in touch with him so he could see how things were going. He also mentioned something that did not make any sense at the time but later would make complete sense. He simply said, "Remember that your wife is not your enemy."

Throughout the years, I have been able to keep in touch with him from time to time. Every time I meet with him, I seem to pick up something new. I was grateful to have him in my life as I needed all the help I could get. His advice helped me to know what to look for and ways I could start to engage the process. He had knowledge and experience about missions that I certainly lacked. He had been a missionary for many years and had a connection with Latin America. I felt blessed and encouraged right away.

He recommended the books *The Insanity of God* and later *The Insanity of Obedience*, written by Nik Ripkin. These two books helped me to put the idea of persecution and obedience in perspective as I moved forward. Many of the stories from these two books were heartbreaking but, at the same time, showed hope. Persecution was something that God was using to build faith and character. Evidence of this type of growth is the highest where persecution is the most intense. The results are expressed in personal growth individually and collectively as a body of believers. Persecution also resulted in large numbers being added to the faith.

Even though I was moving forward by faith, not everything was a bed of roses. One of my biggest struggles came with my wife, Colleen. My faith was increasing as I was obedient to accept God's challenge. Sometimes in relationships, people see things differently, especially in a marriage. The person that I loved the most had a hard time accepting this decision. I did not remember right away about being told my wife is not my enemy as I make decisions.

Colleen is a planner by nature. She likes to have things

organized. She has always looked at the steps to get from Point A to Point B and how to develop them. She had always been that way. She needed order in things. She saw the need to move into doing mission work and had a calling herself early on. Now that, suddenly, I jumped on board, she was skeptical, and rightfully so. She had been praying for me for so long to serve in ministry with her. It was probably a shock to her system to see her prayer answered. It was a long time coming and it was a radical move.

Sometimes I saw that Colleen and I thought about things differently. In general, men and women do think about things differently, but there seemed to be much more than that. The decision to quit my job only amplified these tensions and differences. I initially saw this increase in tension as a form of mistrust on her part. I did not feel respected. Later, I did admit that my actions showed a lack of trust in her. At the time, I was merely looking at her response. I missed the bigger picture. I also admitted I was quite zealous, but over time my attitudes about missions and life, in general, have changed dramatically.

Initially, I felt an adversarial role with Colleen. It was like a black cloud was hanging over us. This was something that caught me completely off guard. I did not catch the idea that my wife was not against me because of our disagreements. Again, I was several steps behind Colleen. I was eager and willing but needed some restraint.

I did lament the fact that I had wasted so many years not appreciating what God had given me. I had not always consulted Him on many decisions. In fact, God always knows what is best for me. It is the Father who always has my best interest at heart. I had made quite a few choices based on circumstances and what looked good to me. I gave that to God and repented of my past unbelief and ungratefulness.

I wanted to move forward. I also wanted to take care of this rift between Colleen and me. As I continued to move forward, I saw a change in my heart toward Colleen. I no longer saw her as someone who was against me. We still had differing opinions about things but that now seemed okay. However, we did see different avenues to pursue ministry. There was still tension in the air, and I was baffled about how to deal with it. I felt paralyzed at times because of our disagreement regarding possible avenues to pursue ministry. I did not want our rift to become a chasm that we could not recover from.

I prayed a lot and asked God to reveal Himself to me and to Colleen. One night, I woke up from a dead sleep and it hit me: we were both right. At first, that seemed so contradictory. She was not the enemy. I knew my wife loved God and she wanted to hear from Him.

The more I looked at our lives, the more I realized we were not all that different. Growing up we had the same insecurities. We both had callings but did not obey those callings until later in our lives. We both had grown up in the church knowing about God but never committing our lives to Jesus until age eighteen. We had often made decisions based on emotions or what looked good instead of consulting the Father. We were more alike than I thought.

The more I began to ponder this, the more it started to make sense. Somehow, we were going to weave all this together. Our different experiences from around the world were going to make a kind of tapestry.

I also heard *do not give up*. My responsibility was to love Colleen even when she disagreed with me. I was to love her as Christ loves the church. I needed to look at where God was working in her life instead of looking at things that I felt needed to change. I needed encouragement as the spiritual leader of the household—a role that I did not take on from the beginning of our marriage. I soon began to understand that Colleen wanted me to be the spiritual leader from the very beginning of our relationship. I took so long stepping into that role; I am sure it frightened her. What I should have been doing my entire Christian walk, I had neglected.

Putting myself in her shoes, I started to see how she might doubt such a radical change. I often thought of Saul's radical change to Paul on the road to Damascus. In the book of Acts, Paul was on his way to deliver some letters to have Christians detained or possibly executed. He wanted to eradicate all Christians and considered them heretics. By eliminating Christians, Paul believed he could squelch the idea that Jesus was the Son of God and had risen from the dead. He was so radically changed by God on his way to Damascus that many were skeptical.

After his experience on the road to Damascus, he now wanted to serve the living Christ. He now endorsed, wholeheartedly, the Christian faith. This type of radical change only comes from God.

Colleen has made the statement to others that the changes in me have reminded her of a Saul-to-Paul conversion. The reality is that all believers should have some element of the Saul-to-Paul change. Not everyone's story will be as dramatic as Paul's. Mine was not. It took many years of failing and missing the mark even after I had accepted Christ as my Savior. It is not our work but the work of the Holy Spirit that changes us. I still have not arrived—reaching for perfection but never attaining it. It is called sanctification (set apart and becoming holy).

The point is that each Christian should be changing in the way he/she thinks. It is a renewing process that can only take place by relying on the Holy Spirit, reading the Word, staying in community, and dying to yourself each day. Our identity needs to be in Christ and Christ alone. This is the transformed life. This is the Gospel that makes a difference. To become more and more like Jesus every day. Jesus said,

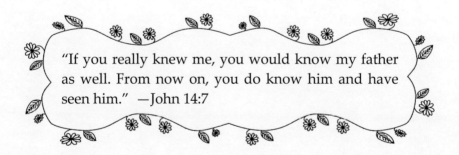

"If you really knew me, you would know my father as well. From now on, you do know him and have seen him." —John 14:7

Abiding is the key. Abiding will drive us to action (obedience) because we know who God is and what He has called us to do.

7

Buenos Dias

A s I continued praying about all this and other things, I began to see that we needed to sell our house and get out of debt. At the time, we were planning another excursion. We planned on checking out VidaNet, a mission in Costa Rica. VidaNet is a Christian mission that trains and equips disciples to know Jesus and live a life that is exemplified by His teachings and ways. VidaNet's vision is to develop community outreach and build relationships with churches. We would be staying for two weeks to check out VidaNet and their discipleship school. Before leaving we put our house up for sale. Our daughter, Meghan, planned to go with us, so there was an anticipation that she might go into ministry with us.

Our local church supported the missionary from Costa Rica that ran the discipleship school as well as other ministries under the umbrella of VidaNet. We had met this missionary at our church before. He spoke about the discipleship process and how VidaNet trained and equipped believers to get them out of their comfort zone. He had affected thousands of people who had come through the doors of VidaNet. Training and equipping others for service in ministry was his passion. We saw some elements of discipleship in his program but wanted an on-the-ground experience of this process—boots on the ground, so to speak.

Costa Rica provided the backdrop to learn about culture and about a process of discipleship. In February 2014, Colleen, Meghan, and I went to Costa Rica for two weeks to check out VidaNet ministries. Right away we could see that Costa Rica lived up to its billing as a country with a rich history. Costa Rican beaches, rain forests, volcanoes, and biodiversity were just a few of its assets. We were surprised that Costa Rica did not have a military. As a result, the government invested huge amounts of money into their education system and health care system. Their literacy rate is quite high. Because Costa Rica does not have a military and the poor outnumber the rich and middle class, some still seem to see Costa Rica as a third-world country or developing country. Despite this misperception, Costa Rica was quite safe, and we could see it was rising in status. By and large, the country seemed remarkably high tech and the standard of living was good for most.

In general, most Costa Ricans are very polite. So polite that for three years in a row their country had been voted the "most friendly county" in the world. Being friendly is a trademark of Costa Rica. Sometimes the locals are so friendly that they would try to help even if they did not know the answer to your question. "Pura Vida" is a marque saying that everyone knew. It is the pure life, the uncomplicated life. Life in general was driven by relationships and connections with others. Life did seem simpler, less complicated.

Driving around the cities we saw the contrasts of the highly populated urban areas versus the smaller, quaint cities. In the bigger cities, traffic was quite congested but public transportation was well developed. Parking always seemed to be an issue. We visited a mall in Alajuela that rivaled any mall that I had ever seen in the US. It was six stories tall and had many retail vendors that carried specialty items. One store sold as many kinds of sweetened hazelnut-cocoa spreads as you can dream of. There were many more specialty stores that had more options than is ever needed.

The biggest city, San José, offered many cultural experiences in the fine arts, opera, historical sites, cuisine, and many retail shops or stores. This is in stark contrast to most of the rest of Costa Rica.

Driving around in the smaller cities would reveal houses that had cement walls around them topped with razor wire and the driveways to the houses had gates or doors. To visit a home, we would need to hit a buzzer to gain entrance. Roads were very narrow, and parking was always an issue due to tight spaces and availability. Driving in Costa Rica was always a challenge as traffic laws seemed optional at times. On the road, things were very spread out and many vendors sold fresh fruits and vegetables along the roadside. Coffee, bananas, pineapples, and sugar plantations dotted the landscape.

Most of the communities have a large church as a reference point. Most of these churches are Catholic. The Catholic church influences much of Latin America, including Costa Rica. The Catholic church did influence a lot of the culture and life of Costa Rica, but VidaNet wanted to use their influence to build up the young people of Costa Rica to be disciples of Christ rather than just attending and identifying with a church building. The discipleship school also used their influence to host short-term teams to educate North American churches and other churches about the discipleship process cross-culturally. VidaNet's goal was to teach that the heart of God is to reach all nations for his glory.

As far as our accommodations, we stayed at the VidaNet base in Heredia. A lot of the ministry took place at the base. Living at the base, we got a glimpse of what discipleship might look like, a sneak preview of things to come. Community was especially important. With the staff and students, there were about twenty-five people living in the base compound. We relied on one another and worked together as a team, cooking, cleaning, and doing general upkeep. It was like a beehive, as there was always something going on.

Communication from the base to the United States was not the best as the internet was spotty at times. While at the base we received an offer on our house. Communication was an issue as the base did not have a fax machine. Our realtor was able to send us electronic communication with an offer on the house. We were able to extend the contract so that we could sign it once we returned to the United States. The housing market was at an all-time low in the States and many friends we knew had their homes on the market for months, some even years. Our home sold within one month. People often asked me, "How did you sell your home so fast?" I had nothing to do with it. It was God; it was simply the grace of God.

We learned a lot about Costa Rican culture and how the discipleship process might work. The discipleship school was called Vida 220. This school trained and equipped future leaders to catch God's vision to glorify Him by deepening a disciple's faith and knowledge of Jesus. The "220" part of "Vida" stemmed from Galatians 2:20.

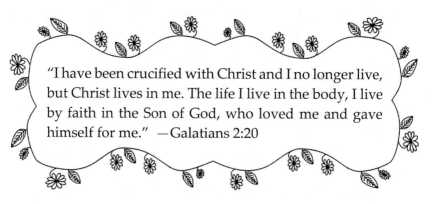

"I have been crucified with Christ and I no longer live, but Christ lives in me. The life I live in the body, I live by faith in the Son of God, who loved me and gave himself for me." —Galatians 2:20

This was a foundational verse that the school would go back to time and time again. Dying to yourself means you are willing to be a servant and follow Jesus despite the costs. Dying to yourself is critical in surrendering to Christ.

Building upon Galatians 2:20, the school taught leaders how to gain a better understanding of how a disciple learns more about Christ and how to obey what is learned. Spiritual disciplines of dying to self, studying the Bible, prayer, the Holy Spirit, spiritual giftings, and building community are developed during a ten-month process. Three months of teachings introduce the discipleship process and what it means to be a disciple of Jesus. The next five months are spent on outreach, connecting with and ministering to churches in various areas of Costa Rica. The last two months are focused on training and equipping short-term team leaders and their youth groups.

Colleen, Meghan, and I were able to join the teachings on how to develop a personal ministry and develop community-kingdom growth. We also studied several books of the Bible to increase our knowledge as well as how to put in practice what we had learned. During this process, we were able to hang out with a lot of the students and build relationships with them. We enjoyed their testimonies and how God was working in their lives to encourage them in possible ministry.

El Nido (the nest) is another part of the VidaNet ministry that addressed issues with pregnant mothers and families. This part of the ministry helped strengthen and build up families by providing physical necessities and counseling services for single mothers. Working with the family unit was integral to developing strong and healthy families.

Working with *El Nido*, Colleen, Meghan, and I helped with an outreach in La Cuenca, commonly referred to as the "pit." Many Nicaraguans fled to Costa Rica due to the economic disparity. Despite this, many Nicaraguans were looked down upon and still lived in poverty. We assisted teachers in working with Nicaraguan refugee children in one of the poorest parts of Costa Rica in the inner city.

We played games and taught Bible lessons and we also provided snacks. The children were so happy to see us, and they participated with great enthusiasm. The smiles on the children's faces were in sharp contrast to their living conditions. It was sad to see that a giant wall had been built so that tourists visiting the mall could not see the area La Cuenca because of its appalling living conditions. VidaNet had an ongoing connection with La Cuenca to provide support and to show the love of Christ to the least of these.

One other ministry of VidaNet was called DaVida. This program did outreach that connected students with various churches to strengthen them so that they (the church) could be a catalyst for change. Building relationships with churches naturally builds community. The church community showed the love and power of God to people who desperately want and need the Good

News. These church communities also loved one another through the riches that Christ had given them. The church communities were then strengthened to become a more living dynamic representation of Jesus. This dynamic representation then affected the entire surrounding community.

The picture was coming into focus, but we still had a lot to learn. However, it was starting to take shape, much like a puzzle. I love jigsaw puzzles—not knowing the complete picture but moving forward so that things start to take shape. God was not only letting us know that discipleship was a process but that there would be a cost. Discipleship is hard work and does not happen overnight, but God is faithful. We seemed to be gaining valuable insight and connections along the journey. We were seeing the beginnings of living life-on-life done in different cultures.

We finished our experience in Costa Rica with more studying, outreach, worshipping God, and building community.

On an outreach in Talamanca (a province of Limon), Colleen learned a valuable lesson about ministry. She often did not know the purpose of what we were doing. In Talamanca, she was asked, "What can you do to connect with the ladies here?" The question caught Colleen by surprise. Colleen knew how to cross-stitch, but she was not sure how that would fit in. She did not have any of the necessary equipment or material to cross-stitch. It was not a coincidence that some North American missionaries had the equipment she was looking for. It made her think about ministry and the need to just look for opportunities and believe that God would supply all her needs. She had so much fun teaching how to cross-stitch and just connecting with people.

It was like that throughout our time in Costa Rica, not always knowing but always hoping. Getting snapshots but not the whole picture. We did see that ministry is difficult work and can be exhausting. Being flexible was something we had to get used to but was an essential part of doing any ministry.

Being a missionary is not a bed of roses as it is often portrayed to be. There are often setbacks and obstacles along the way.

Discipleship is often messy as you deal with people's personal issues as well as your own. We were getting a bigger picture of the "good, the bad, and the ugly." We started to see that doing ministry was hard work and required a specific focus of energy. We were not busy just doing things, but we did discover that discipleship did take effort and perseverance.

Another connecting point for discipleship was teaching English as a Second Language (ESL). ESL could help build community as well as expand available options. At the time, the average Costa Rican's income was about six hundred dollars a month. In comparison, Costa Rica's neighbor Nicaragua averaged about forty dollars a month. If Costa Ricans learned English, they could possibly double their average monthly income. Many Costa Ricans who knew English were working for call centers or with American businesses. Learning English was a way of investing in the welfare of Costa Rica by providing upward mobility. We attended an English conversational group that opened our minds about teaching English as a tool to connect with others. Costa Ricans were so eager to learn English. We saw it as such a great connecting point.

It was an awesome experience visiting Costa Rica and getting our feet wet. We learned so much in Costa Rica but there seemed to be so much more to learn. This idea of community kept coming up over and over. We started to see a vision of discipleship done within the community context. Discipleship moves at the speed of relationships in community. We had seen church community before but had never seen the discipleship process done in community quite like that.

8

Macedonia, Here We Come Again

W e went back to the United States again having gained a creative look at the discipleship process. Our daughter really enjoyed herself and was grappling with what missions might look like and what her role could be. We started to pray about the next step.

I (Armin) felt we needed to go back to Macedonia as there just seemed to be something that was left undone. I could not quite put my finger on exactly what that meant. I knew it would not be a long-term thing. Nevertheless, I kept getting this gnawing feeling that something was left undone. We connected with CCC staff and decided to return to Macedonia a second time.

During our second stay in Macedonia, we ministered at the youth camp doing a third Speak Out. Again, our daughter went with us. She worked well with the children and I saw her possibly doing some type of children's ministry. This third Speak Out was quite different than the first go-round; it was much more structured. There was more emphasis on training and developing a strategy to engage others. There was much more importance placed on the Gospel and how to share it. We learned the Four Spiritual Laws (four biblical principles about sharing Jesus's love with others) and how to share our testimonies. It was all done in community.

We had life groups with the youth all week long.

Later, we would plan fun activities to do with the youth. We also took time each day to practice English-speaking skills with the campers. Some of them spoke English well but wanted to add words to their vocabulary. They were eager to learn more English. Many Macedonians learned English by watching movies in English. Teaching English, even if it was mainly vocabulary, was a way to connect. We saw how using English was an icebreaker and the campers began to relax and trust us more.

As trust was built, we started to work on our long testimonies with the CCC staff. I shared my testimony with the staff for review and to give feedback. This was the long version of my testimony, so it took a lot of thought and effort to organize it. My testimony was well received. Then came the bad news. The problem was that my testimony would fit well in an American context. The staff felt it would be a great testimony back in the United States, but not in Macedonia.

I had focused on the calling to quit my job and how God had provided all the way. In the Macedonian context, it certainly would seem foolish and unwise to quit a job, even if things did work out. Macedonia had an unemployment rate of nearly 31 percent, and it had been that high for years. The economy had severely deteriorated and many people were desperate. It made no sense to quit a job, faith or no faith.

I was thankful that the staff were frank with me and were willing to share the truth. In love, they gave me feedback so that I could have a more effective witness. Their honesty was commendable. That was my introduction to contextualization (to place something, such as a word or activity, in a context). No longer could I think in terms of what I knew and perceived through my western American lens; I would need to share my faith as looking through the viewpoint of another's culture. Each culture has its own unique view of life, but the Word of God is truth and we must not compromise it.

I had worked hard on my testimony and now I had to scrap it. We were supposed to share our testimony with our group the next day. There was not enough time to develop a new testimony. I felt helpless and defeated for a moment. I quickly prayed that the Holy Spirit would give me something to say, as I had nothing at this point.

Early the next day, we met with our life group. The theme of broken family relations was discussed earlier in the day and we were to continue that discussion in our small groups later in the afternoon. Without much thought, I figured I would share a family story about restoration and forgiveness. I told the Macedonian youth the story of how my father came to Christ. I indicated that my father had not known Christ most of his life. In 2008, my mother went into the hospital and things did not look good. My dad was in a visiting room by himself. My brother and I shared Christ with him and prayed with him. We knew it was a difficult thing to see our mother looking death in the face.

We knew Dad would feel alone if Mom died. We had been praying for many years that my mom and dad would come to know Christ. Nothing happened at that point, but we did all that could be done for the moment. We had shared again with Mom and Dad and nothing happened. Mom died shortly after that. Two weeks later, I received a call from my dad. He proclaimed, "I did it." Now my first inclination was to think, *Oh no, what did my dad do?* He had accepted Christ. I was so thrilled to hear those words.

Tears were rolling down my cheek as I was telling the story to the Macedonian youth. Our family had just about given up and God delivered my father. The next part of the story blew the kids out of the water. My dad asked if I remembered the day at the hospital when my brother and I had shared about Christ with him. He said, "If you boys hadn't intervened with hope that night, I surely would have killed myself. I had every intention of doing so and had planned to do it that night. You and your brother made me think a lot and it stopped me from killing myself." I had assumed that nothing happened. God was indeed working out my father's salvation.

From that point on I have had a totally different relationship with my dad. The best thing was that he realized that he needed

God's grace and forgiveness and he was willing to accept what Jesus did for him at the cross. He asked for my forgiveness for never telling me my whole life that he loved me. He never hugged me. He had never received love like that from his father. He had loved me like his dad had loved him—loving but not actually saying it with words or with a simple hug. He simply did not know how to love in that way. Christ made all the difference in the world.

I saw a transformation in my dad. I knew he would not be perfect, but I did see he had a purpose. He knew God in a way that made him valuable despite any shortcomings. He now hugs me when I see him and tells me that he loves me. He wanted to go to church with Colleen and me. My prayers had been answered in more than one way; talk about the Spirit moving. God impressed upon me that being prepared is important but relying on the spirit is much more important to reach the hearts of others.

On another front, Meghan and Colleen helped tutor several of the youth who lived about ten minutes away. They practiced English with them and shared the Gospel as well. Two of the girls were Orthodox Christians, so Colleen and Meghan learned more about the Christian Orthodox viewpoint. Another seed planted. From that camp experience, there were several who gave their lives to Christ and many more who were undecided about their faith.

One of the young boys stood out from the rest of the campers. He had attended the second Speak Out the previous year and had returned this year for the third Speak Out. On his previous Speak Out, he was one of the more vocal "campers." He was adamant that he did not like the experience. At the time, he said there was no God. He was furious that his dad was unemployed. He completed the Speak Out but many of the staff believed that due to his poor attitude and general dislike of God that they would never see him again. God moves in mysterious ways. He signed up for the next Speak Out as a camper again and the staff were quite shocked.

The staff made special mention to warn me about his behavior and issues from the previous year. He would be assigned to my table. I had anticipated that his attitude would be much the same from the year before. To my surprise, I found him to be one of the most interesting and congenial campers. So much so that I knew God had to be working in his life. He had a lot of good questions and was engaged with the overall process. I saw little of the negativity that the staff had reported from last year. I prayed a lot for him and took extra time to engage him as best as I could.

I could tell that he was close to accepting Christ, but something was holding him back. I later found out that there was some follow-up done with him by the staff from CCC. Interestingly, he would return again for a fourth Speak Out the next year. The staff were at a loss for what to do with him. He kept coming back but he refused to decide to accept Christ. The staff questioned his motives as it appeared that he was only attending the Speak Out to socialize or hang out.

The staff tried a new approach. They reversed the roles and asked him how he would respond if a nonbeliever had faith questions. They had him help with the campers for that year. It was amazing. Somehow, that role reversal forced him to think differently and he finally accepted Christ. He would go on to partner with them for several years and help with the CCC ministry. His story and my dad's story reminded me that no one is beyond hope. Even when we think God is not working; He is faithful, and He will do the things that seem impossible.

Another way of building community was by living with the missionaries. Colleen and I stayed with the staff in their apartment, living life-on-life. We were getting to know them more intimately. We observed how missionaries live on a day-to-day basis. We started to know them better by being with them. That is truly God's heart; He wants us to know Him by being with Him. He wants us to spend quality time with Him daily.

As we were doing "life-on-life" with the staff, we would visit traditional sites and places of interest. We visited some of the Orthodox churches and found the architecture to be stunning. The detail and grandeur took my breath away. The representations of the different saints were spectacular. Candles and icons were everywhere. Many of the beautiful mosaics told Bible stories. One of the mosaics was a detailed account of Paul's journeys. The details were quite impressive. However, despite all the fanfare, there seemed to be an emptiness that I could not shake.

As I passed the threshold of one of the churches, I immediately felt a staleness and an emptiness. It was strange to see all the beauty and wonder of the church building but feel a lack of life. I did struggle with this as I knew the church was important to the Macedonians. I started to think about the words of Jesus.

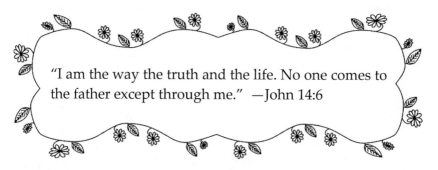

"I am the way the truth and the life. No one comes to the father except through me." —John 14:6

The word *life* was so important. Then it hit me. The church building was not the source of life—Jesus was life. Many Christians have identified with the building itself as the source or place of their worship. Jesus is, in fact, the Way, the Truth, and the Life. As we finished hanging out with the missionaries we returned to Greece once again. We had another wonderful time experiencing places that brought us back to biblical times.

At the end of the trip, we drove to a village in Macedonia in which the Romas lived. These Romas were Gypsies with Indian ancestry. They were despised and considered the lowest of the low. These Gypsies lived in the most impoverished areas and were known for begging and using their children to get money. The men would often abuse the women if they did not beg or find a way to get money. The Gypsies were considered the dregs of society. They were the untouchables.

We were able to visit with some of those untouchables and share the love of Christ with them. We were reaching out to those who felt hopeless, lost to Macedonia and to God. We were connecting with "the least of these." Again, more seeds were planted.

We finished up strong and started to feel that things were coming together. We were beginning to see the discipleship process in ways that equipped us to teach others how to be a disciple. As always, we still had questions, but we were moving forward. By the grace of God, some things were starting to come into focus.

9

Developing a Strategy

A fter returning to Ohio, Colleen and I began to think about our next step. We thought about what mission agency we should join. The missionary in Costa Rica had been working with Globe International as his mission agency. It seemed to be the next logical step for us to investigate Globe as a possible mission agency.

In 2014, we decided to join Globe's team. We attended their missionary candidacy school. We went through the basics in starting up a mission (cross-culturally) and familiarizing ourselves with the policies and procedures of Globe. As we still had not picked a particular people group to minister to, our mentor from Globe requested that we visit the small city of Clarkston, Georgia. Clarkston is a city of about thirteen thousand residents and is located seven and a half miles east of Atlanta, Georgia.

In Clarkston, there is a mission agency called Global Frontier Missions (GFM). GFM has a history of success working with refugees, immigrants, and internationals. GFM's focus is on sharing the Gospel with refugees and other internationals. They also help foreigners to assimilate and to learn English. GFM operates a school to train missionaries for field service abroad and to engage international communities.

We stopped and visited with the chief executive officer of GFM. In 2000, he started GFM and began serving in southern Mexico. In 2009, he launched a ministry hub in Clarkston, Georgia. He gave us a brief history of Clarkston. Clarkston is an area the United Nations and the United States has designated as a refugee resettlement area. Clarkston had become quite diverse over the years and at the time, refugees were pouring in by the hundreds each month. There were more than sixty nations represented in a one-square-mile area, making it the most diverse square mile in all the United States. In addition to the Missionary Training School (MTS), GFM also offered training to short-term teams from all around the country. We reported our contact to our mentor at Globe International.

There was something intriguing about Clarkston; it was an amazingly unique city. GFM's goal was to train missionaries and send them out to the nations. The crazy thing was that the nations were being sent to Clarkston and other areas of the country. It seemed to be a good training ground to learn more about cross-cultural missions. We went back to Ohio with a glimpse of an area in the United States that had great potential for cross-cultural training. It also had great potential to reach the nations due to its diversity.

Our next step was to complete several required readings about missions and to attend a mission course called "Perspectives." In this course, we learned about the heart of missions, mission history, mission's development, and more practical steps we could take to move forward in the mission field. We listened to several missionaries share their experiences on the field. We also learned about cutting-edge missions, new developments, and strategies to reach those who need the Gospel.

We took the intensive form of the classes, so the whole course was crammed into one week. It was hard work and there was a ton of homework. After completing the course, we worked on finishing all the required readings for Perspectives. We studied hard and passed tests in each section. We also wrote a paper on how to develop a strategy to engage unreached people who had been caught up in sex trafficking and slavery. In about three months we finally completed everything to obtain a certificate.

After finishing Perspectives, we continued to pray for the next step. We were thinking about Costa Rica, but something caught my eye about Clarkston. If we had not figured out a particular people group to go to, then maybe Clarkston would hold the answer. It was diversity on steroids. GFM had a summer internship program that would give us more exposure to different cultures, and we would be trained to host short-term mission teams. We could get trained in a cross-cultural setting without even leaving the US.

That summer, as interns, Colleen and I spent a lot of time with other interns that were mainly in their twenties. We all learned so much about culture. Colleen and I also learned a lot from the twenty-somethings. We had no idea from day-to-day what kind of culture we might encounter. It was so dynamic; it made my head spin.

My first experience in Clarkston was an eye-opener. We all took the GFM van to tour the city. The idea was to familiarize ourselves with the different areas of Clarkston. For one-square-mile, that did not take a lot of effort.

As I looked out the van window, I saw a lot of kids wearing different clothes. They were all in a line walking on the sidewalk. I asked, "What's the parade for?" Everyone in the van started roaring with laughter. Except for me. All the kids were walking home from school wearing traditional outfits from the country they came from. "Clarkston 101, baby."

Clarkston is so diverse that the first time I visited it, I thought I had stepped into the Twilight Zone. Not only is Clarkston diverse, but it is an area where a lot of other mission agencies are doing ministry. There is a lot of activity going on in that one-square-mile. As well, there were approximately sixty nations represented in that one-square-mile. There were over one-hundred-plus dialects spoken by students in the school system.

I later found out that the county (Dekalb) in which Clarkston is located is the most diverse county in the United States. I could travel around the world and never meet as many internationals. GFM trained us in basic cross-cultural etiquette and how to adapt the Gospel accordingly. We began to see the value of missions in a new light and how the Gospel could reach the nations, even while living in the States. Again, we were seeing how relationships and building community are vitally important.

Although it was fun and we learned a lot, my wife and I are not spring chickens. We were quite a bit older than all the other interns, and we were the only married couple. The young adults had energy that we did not. I often referred to us as crash-test dummy pilots. We were tired and lacked energy, but God was gracious to help us finish. Once we finished the training, we hosted short-term teams from across the United States. The goal was to train each team and have them take a vision back to their local church or community. In addition, we hoped the training might possibly inspire a few to do cross-cultural missions work; maybe even some might want to attend the mission training school. Again, the schedule and pace were difficult, but God was our comforter and sustainer.

GFM partnered with Friends of Refugees to further build community relationships. Friends of Refugees was the original mission agency that helped refugees assimilate to the US culture in the 1990s. Working with Friends of Refugees, we picked an area in which we wanted to serve the refugee population. Each area would serve as a smaller team to work with the refugee community.

My area was the Clarkston Community Garden. The garden was created to develop a sense of community and enhance the refugee's sense of belonging. The idea of the community garden was for refugees to pay a small fee to have a garden plot and grow whatever they wanted, if it was legal.

As I served in the garden, it did not go quite as expected, but I loved working there. Our team members served to provide support, get necessary tools and other supplies the refugees might need. There was always a lot of cleanup. Work needed to be done to organize, improve the system, and keep people safe. The staff was not there to tell the refugees how to garden or what to plant; our team simply maintained an environment that helped them to manage their garden plot. Other short-term teams from around the area would join our team throughout the summer to work on bigger projects. The garden staff also provided education tours of the facility to enhance community awareness and build community connections. There was a lot of activity in the garden.

One funny story that I want to share came from the garden experience. The leader of the garden had told me that I could take trash and drop it off in some dumpsters just outside the community garden. I was handpicked to keep tabs on a young man who was doing community service hours (on probation) at the garden. I guess I was chosen because I worked in law enforcement in Ohio and that somehow made me perfect for the job. I took this young man with me to deliver the trash to the dumpsters outside the garden area.

On our third visit, I noticed a police officer standing beside the dumpster. I had a bad feeling in the pit of my stomach. The officer indicated that someone in the apartment complex had called the police department about illegal dumping. How embarrassing! I worked in law enforcement and had someone on probation with me. It was an awkward moment. The situation was finally resolved, and God was gracious to us. Because of the work of the Friends of Refugees in the community and at the garden, the officer was willing to give the young man and me a break. The officer gave us a stern warning but did not file charges against us for illegal dumping. The stern warning was not to come back into the neighborhood. Violating that order could result in going to jail.

Colleen picked the Friends of Refugee Summer Camp as her smaller outreach team. Colleen worked much harder than I did. She worked with youth all summer long. It takes a lot of energy to work with youth, more energy than she had. There were a lot of kids from various backgrounds. No two days were alike. It was exhausting, both physically and mentally. Many days she would come home and just crash. There were days when she wanted to give up and quit. However, she remained faithful to finish what God had started. Every day, she would come home with a new story of conflict and how the staff handled the situation. There was conflict almost every day.

One story that was memorable involved two boys who had just moved to Clarkston. They were from different African refugee camps. They were from different countries, but they had one thing in common: despite living in different refugee camps, they spoke the same language. They were now living in a totally foreign country and were having trouble adjusting.

One day, the boys were talking to each other and a verbal fight broke out between the two of them. The other counselor and Colleen knew if they sent the boys to the director of the camp, both were going to be expelled. They decided to take the boys away from the group and talk to them one on one in the garden that was in the corner of the camp. God works in mysterious ways.

As they started talking, both boys let their guard down and started reminiscing about their homeland. They were able to resolve their differences and forgive each other. The garden seemed to provide a safe zone that would enable the boys to calm down and give them an opportunity to be vulnerable so healing could occur. It was a stroke of genius.

Throughout the summer, campers were exposed to Bible themes which helped to address many of the conflicts and helped them to develop character. God gave Colleen the grace to persevere and truly help the kids. It was hard work, but it was rewarding to know she was making a difference in their lives.

One other issue that came up during the summer internship was helping versus hurting. It seemed that due to the constant flow of short-term teams during the summer, relationships with the refugees were being developed and then terminated just as quickly. We saw evidence of that firsthand.

A young adult from one of the teams would go out with Colleen and me on outreach every day. Colleen and I had already developed a relationship with a Burmese family so we thought that would be a good place to start. All week long we visited with that Burmese family. The family started to take a liking to the young adult. We could see that she was connecting with the children of the family. On her last day visiting, she announced that she would be leaving the next day. She said, "It will be okay because Armin and Colleen will be here the rest of the summer." The young adult had been there less than a week. One of the Burmese boys put his head down; he was heartbroken. We never saw him again.

Well, the debate went on about helping versus hurting. Due to recognizing the problem and subsequent discussion about it, GFM changed their approach for short-term mission teams. It was a hard lesson learned, but a good one.

One of the other things that I enjoyed as an intern was a time referred to as the "Harvest Week." During this time, GFM specifically prayed to meet a person of peace or a house of peace, understanding that the Lord was over the harvest. The leaders of GFM would take the interns out and knock on doors. Knocking on doors is a real, intentional way of meeting people but it does take some time to get used to. The specific purpose was to find a person or house of peace and engage them with the message (Gospel) of peace. A person of peace is a person who accepts the messenger, the message of the Gospel, and the mission of God's plan for the redemption of all people. Once this person of peace accepted the mission of God, they became a stream through which the Gospel could flow. It would flow through their established contacts and natural relations.

I went out with one of the leaders of GFM. He would later become our team leader when we would return in 2018. He had a way about him, and he seemed dependent on the Lord to do the job. During the Harvest Week, we came across a house of peace. It was no accident. We were initially sharing with a man who needed a job and healing for his arm. We were also handing out DVDs of a film about Jesus. We had just finished praying and started to walk around the corner when I heard a faint voice say, "Can I have one of those DVDs?" We were just seconds away from turning the corner and missing this contact completely; it was God's timing all the way.

As soon as we entered the house, we both sensed that something big was going to happen. We engaged a married couple from Africa who were Christians. They had been in the United States for many years. However, they had been beaten down by medical, spiritual, and other issues. They had fallen so far down that they seemed to have lost their purpose. They seemed helpless and lost. We prayed for them for deliverance from all these issues. It was intense. There were a lot of issues. Before we knew it, several hours had passed. We saw the African couple come to life. They had smiles on their faces when before it was sadness. They had a bounce in their step that was lacking just hours before. We encouraged them to get back in the Word and to start praying about connecting with other believers. We also wanted them to know that we believed they were destined to change their neighborhood. This couple was able to get connected with others and they were greatly strengthened and encouraged.

Later, I returned to find out that they were able to rent the apartment on the end of their building complex with the help of a mission agency in Clarkston. This couple used the apartment to help kids stay off the street after school. They provided English as a Second Language (ESL) classes. They also provided snacks and other items for the kids. You could tell that they loved kids and were making a huge difference.

Checking on them from time to time, I discovered the whole story. I met with the husband and he told me that his wife did not trust white people when we first arrived. He was surprised at the time that his wife had let us in the door during Harvest Week. He believed it was because we presented a peace that could only come from God. There had been such an overwhelming sense of peace that they both knew that God had sent us to minister to them. They immediately knew that we were people of God. Since that time, they wanted to be people of peace wherever they went. Their lifelong goal was now to spread peace. Honestly, we had nothing to do with it other than being available and listening for the Lord's leading to show us to a house of peace. We just knew the Lord would be faithful. Their response greatly encouraged us and the Clarkston community.

One other contact on outreach was also noteworthy. We were serving with several interns walking the neighborhoods in Clarkston. As we were walking in the Clarkston Oaks apartment complex, we saw two Muslims sitting at a picnic table. We decided to talk with them.

At first, the conversation revolved around God being holy and that He was like no other God. We told them we were Jesus followers and wanted to spend time just getting to know them. As we talked, I could see that they seemed to hold God in high regard. Somewhere along the line, the conversation changed. The two Muslims told us their story of converting from Christianity to Islam. I felt a pit in my stomach as they shared their conversion from Christianity. They were very scholarly and seemed to have a lot of the answers. They soon became hostile toward us. They mentioned that they knew who we were and that our goal was to convert them. I interjected that our goal was not to convert anyone. That was God's business. We just wanted to show Jesus, plain and simple. This changed the whole dynamics of the conversation and we dialogued about many different topics. To them, knowledge was everything, so this debate was healthy.

After we finished, one of the Muslims indicated that we were the only Christians who had said that we were not there to convert them. I often thought about his statement. It made me feel sad.

No wonder why people seem hostile at times when we present the Gospel. If our witness just seems to be about converting people, we have missed the mark. I felt our conversation made an impression on them. It certainly made an impression on me. This contact showed me a lot about the Muslim faith and how to begin engaging them. Be yourself and be honest. Admit that you are a Jesus follower and be willing to listen. Pray a lot and do not get caught up in a lot of theological debate. Just show Jesus, plain and simple.

Later, a friend said he had observed us talking to the two Muslims. He asked if I knew who they were. Not sure, I said,

"They were two Muslims who seemed to be informed about their faith and about the Christian faith. They were Christians who had converted to Islam."

My friend said, "That's not it." I was perplexed with his response. He pointed out that those were the two highest-ranking Muslims in that area. My heart skipped a beat. My jaw almost dropped to the floor. God works in mysterious ways. If I had known this information ahead of time, I may have shrunken back from engaging with them. I felt humbled but also more confident. Another seed was planted.

All throughout the summer, the other interns discussed similar contacts and stories of how God was working in Clarkston. GFM and other mission agencies were making an impact for the kingdom of God by reaching out to internationals, refugees, and immigrants with the Gospel of peace.

10

Missionary Boot Camp

W e finished the summer internship with thoughts of possibly attending GFM's missionary training school. By now, I was convinced that we should not make any decisions about our next step until we had consulted the Father. The decision came down to staying in Clarkston or heading back to Costa Rica. We prayed for over a month about this as both options looked good. One thing God had taught me along the way was not to look at things in terms of "good" or "bad." He simply wanted me to connect with Him and get my marching orders directly from Him. Either way, we knew it would be a long-term commitment.

The final decision was made to return to Costa Rica for at least one year and work with the discipleship school (Vida 220) as students and staff members. Our daughter, Meghan, initially planned to go with us. The fundraising effort seemed to be an issue with her. I did not see any effort to raise funds on her part. I wanted her to be invested in the process. I continued to question her on this issue. She thought about it and had changed her mind; she had other aspirations for now. It was hard, but we did not want to pressure Meghan into doing something she was not ready to do. Besides, she was at a point that she would need to start developing her own faith apart from ours. We trusted that we could leave our daughter in the Lord's hands and He was plenty capable of taking care of her. She was the Lord's daughter, not just our daughter.

In May 2016 we traveled to Costa Rica again, this time without

Meghan. Colleen struggled with the separation from Meghan. She also struggled with separation from my dad. She would later feel an uneasiness about not being there for our future daughters-in-law. Both of our boys became engaged and were starting to plan their respective marriages. Colleen's struggle was with relationships that she was missing out on. She somehow felt she had abandoned them. Even so, God did some amazing things while we were in Costa Rica.

Over time, Colleen and I began to enjoy Costa Rica more and more. We enjoyed getting to know the people and developing great relationships. We served the best that we could, even though many times we did not know the next step. Sounds familiar. Our roles were not well-defined, but that did not stop us from just serving well and being available. It was okay because we were learners. Back to the basics again. We can always learn something new every day. From the start, we saw God's blessings.

We joined the team at the VidaNet mission base in San Isidro in the providence of Heredia. However, we did not have a place to stay permanently. We stayed at the base awhile, but we were soon able to move into an apartment about a fifteen-minute walk from the base. We had such good landlords and they were so kind and helpful. Their daughter spoke some English and soon we became good friends with her. From time to time we would also play with her four-year-old son. Within a couple of weeks, our landlord invited us to a party for her grandson's birthday. When they say "party" in Costa Rica, they mean "party." It was so much fun getting to know the family and others. The party went on for hours. After about four hours, we had to leave as we were still on a schedule with things to do. We felt bad that we had left early, but the party still went on without us. Again, relationships were being established, which was especially important.

As far as the school was concerned, Colleen and I were staff and students of the Vida 220 discipleship school. One thing we learned right away was how important discipline was. If you were exactly on time or late to anything you had to do push-ups.

Fortunately for us, this was not a problem. If you forgot your Bible or disobeyed any of the instructions, it was more push-ups. Forgetting your Bible was at the top of the list, costing five hundred push-ups. Sometimes you did deep knee bends. If one of the students could not do all their push-ups, then the community would chip in and do the balance of push-ups. I did a lot more push-ups by chipping in to help others than I did for myself.

As we were getting a good workout, we also helped by providing some basic ESL with the discipleship students. This took us back to our first trip to Costa Rica when we saw the benefit of doing conversational English. We were now beginning to implement that vision. We helped in other areas by just being available to serve. We helped paint, clean up, provide transportation, and assist in any other area where there was a need.

After making a transportation run with the fifteen-passenger van, I met the director of Vida 220. The first thing that I did was complain about the traffic, as it took us several hours more than usual to get back to the base. I was severely chastised for not even saying "Hi" or "How are you doing?" It was rude to act like that no matter what culture I was in; in Costa Rica, it was extremely rude. I had to do a reality check and remember that sometimes my nature was to complain about things. My apology was accepted, and I really began to look at how complaining was an issue that I needed to work on.

As students, we worked on various issues like that. This helped lead us through the discipleship process of dying to self. We also covered more advanced teachings on healing, the Holy Spirit, and the different disciplines of the Christian faith.

One teaching for me was a game-changer. Even though I knew that God loved me, I missed the actual depth of His love. When I looked at God's love in-depth, I discovered that I was still clinging onto good works to reach God. I had so many rules in front of me that I missed God's love again. I finally decided to glorify God by loving Him with all my heart, mind, soul, and strength and then loving others as I love myself. Not in a vain way, but the way

Christ loves us. It changed everything. I now loved God because He first loved me, not the other way around.

"We love because he first loved us." —1 John 4:19

It was now an issue of loving God and becoming more like Him through Christ.

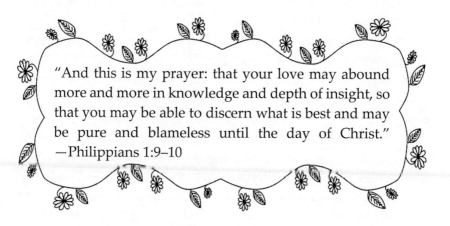

"And this is my prayer: that your love may abound more and more in knowledge and depth of insight, so that you may be able to discern what is best and may be pure and blameless until the day of Christ." —Philippians 1:9–10

It was no longer a matter of trying to do the right thing or trying to gain God's approval. As I loved God and people more, a natural outflow came out of me to be holy, to do the right thing. I discovered this and it opened the door for me to be more genuine, not acting out of obligation. It was becoming a lifestyle. My identity in Christ was becoming stronger. It was a liberating experience to know that if I put God first and then focused on others, I would naturally want to obey Him out of love. There were many other lessons that I learned, but that was a big one.

One way that the discipleship school showed God's love to others was by doing dramas. We participated in the crucifixion drama. I played a Roman soldier. I wanted authenticity and impact, so I played the part with energy and spirit. However, it was Jesus's part that made the most impact. After the drama, we had a time of reflection. Many of the kids mentioned many troubling and disturbing things in their lives. Some were delivered from pornography and drugs/alcohol. Others gave their lives to Christ. It was an immensely powerful drama that had impacted short-term teams in more than one way. Other dramas were practiced by the team and performed on outreach—the same thing happened. It was amazing how God was using these dramas to love and reach people, especially the youth.

God was showing me depth to things that I already knew. Adding depth to things is in God's nature because He is so deep. He also wants to challenge us with new things, so we do not become stale and ineffective. A good friend of mine would say that when a Christian departs from this world, he/she will have eternity to get to know God. To me, this was an amazing statement about heaven. The point is that God's nature and His depth are endless. It was such a pleasure to see God's love in a new light and depth.

I started to think about my children. I thought about how I had disciplined them as they were growing up. I immediately got on the phone and apologized to each of them. I had unwittingly set them up for failure by using the law as a standard for obedience at all costs. When you are under this type of pressure, you find yourself frustrated and become locked into legalism. Also, there is a propensity to change the rules (find loopholes) to keep the original rules at all costs. Loopholes are a means of escape or evasion of the law as it is written. This thinking causes a pressure that God never intended.

I realized that children would follow the rules until they could find a way around them (this also holds true for adults). When my children did not follow the rules, my response had been to change the rules so that they could not circumvent doing the right thing. Following the rule of the law was because I said so. There was no love in that and there certainly was not any grace. I should have been teaching them the heart behind why we obey versus just obeying out of obligation.

Finding loopholes in the law became a way to keep the law and still appear to be righteous. With each loophole encountered, frustration mounted. With my apology and explanation of God's love, I hoped that my children caught the idea that everything flowed from the fact that God loved them first. As a result of that, they would want to love God with all their mind, heart, soul, and strength. Then they would be in a much better position to love others. It would come naturally, not out of obligation.

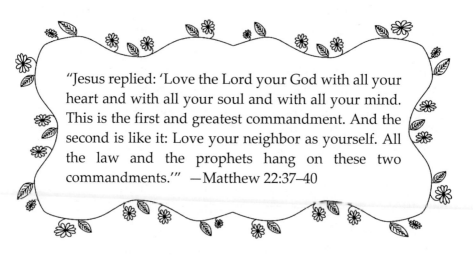

"Jesus replied: 'Love the Lord your God with all your heart and with all your soul and with all your mind. This is the first and greatest commandment. And the second is like it: Love your neighbor as yourself. All the law and the prophets hang on these two commandments.'" —Matthew 22:37–40

As I look at society in general, this is where we are. There are layers and layers of laws because of loopholes, so much so that we have lost the original intent of the law. As well there are so many laws that we cannot possibly follow all of them. We also see a dilemma where guilt and innocence are blurred. A person could now break the law and because of a technicality, be found innocent.

This dilemma reminds me of the Pharisees and Sadducees in the New Testament. They were religious leaders of Jesus's day that wanted to follow the rule of the law of Moses. Their heart was to follow the letter of the law to gain God's approval. Jesus saw this self-righteous behavior and confronted it. Jesus is interested in our heart attitude. Loving the Lord (getting to know Jesus) is so important. In John 15, the word "abide" is mentioned eleven times. As a matter of fact, the phrases "in Christ" and "in Him" are mentioned 164 times in the Epistles (letters to the churches).

As you love Jesus more, you will want to become holy because He is holy. You will also learn there is a judgment; God is holy and cannot stand sin. However, God's forgiveness by grace trumps wrath and judgment. As you begin to love Jesus more and more, your life will soon be directed by more and more of the Holy Spirit and prayer. As you love Jesus and others more, you will see and show the fruit of the Spirit.

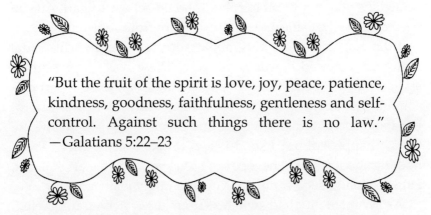

"But the fruit of the spirit is love, joy, peace, patience, kindness, goodness, faithfulness, gentleness and self-control. Against such things there is no law."
—Galatians 5:22–23

As you love Jesus more and more, you will be drawn to community for strength and encouragement. The ultimate outpouring will be through a community that will want to see the nations reached for His name's sake and for His glory.

One other critical lesson I discovered is that you do not have to be competent or well-versed at something to make a difference. I saw Costa Ricans and others playing soccer and I observed that they were having fun and that it brought communities together. One of the local Costa Ricans started a soccer ministry and he was making a big difference. The players were starting to get along with each other better. They were not as consumed with just winning. They started to clean up their language and their attitudes were changing. It was because he took the time to set an example and love them, with no conditions or strings attached. That unconditional love made all the difference.

Costa Ricans enjoy soccer anywhere and would use whatever was available to make a soccer goal. Soccer had a way of connecting people. My problem was that they were so good at soccer. If I tried, I would certainly look like a fool. Besides, I had never even played soccer before. To complicate matters, I was aging "well" and had several health problems. That alone should have stopped me in my tracks from even trying such a thing. As I started to mull this over, it soon came to my mind that I would look like a fool playing soccer. Everyone should expect me to look like a fool. Trying something you know nothing about should be easy to start. All you need do is be available and willing to learn from someone else.

I did not know anything about soccer. I mean zilch! Nada! However, I sensed it would be okay. There was no pressure. I started playing with no expectations other than to be a part of a community. I made it a point to let them know that I knew nothing about soccer but was willing and eager to learn. I am not sure how it happened, but I soon began to like a game that I knew nothing about and had never even tried before. As a matter of fact, I always found soccer quite boring and rarely watched it on TV.

As my mentality had switched from just watching to playing, it opened a door for me I never expected. As I began to play more and more, I felt more relaxed and began to feel more confident and connected. I watched every move of the players and wanted to learn more. I was a learner and they were willing to give me so much grace. I certainly needed it. Being older also helped reduce the expectations as well. I soon found myself practicing every day in my apartment and learning how to control the ball by juggling. It was a miracle that I did not break anything in the apartment.

I soon felt drawn to a game that I had never liked or tried. It was totally crazy. I continued to focus on the relational aspect of the game. I had no aspirations of becoming great at soccer. I, nevertheless, felt drawn to it. I wanted to practice and learn as much as I could.

One day in class, we were doing a lesson about thinking outside the box and thinking big. Soccer kept coming to my mind. I wrote down the words "soccer ministry." I had no idea what that could mean. I had just started learning about this newfound game. It was absolutely the most insane idea I have ever had. I have had a few crazy ideas before but this one seemed to top them all.

I never gave up on that idea; I continued to practice more and play when I could get into a game. All I could do at the time was practice and pray that somehow God would open the door for me. I really needed a mentor to help me along with this process. Playing street soccer was okay, but as far as learning positioning and developing skills as a team player, you can forget about it. In street soccer, mechanics go out the window. It is every man, woman, and child for themselves. I was okay with that for now, but I wanted more. I still had a lot of questions and concerns about how soccer could be used as a ministry. I would continue to think about this off and on for quite some time.

Another good thing that happened in Costa Rica was that Colleen got her ESL certification. My role during that process was to be an encourager and supporter. I also tried to do as much as I could around the house. I knew this would help ease the pressure off Colleen because of the demanding schedule to complete the certification. I was so proud of her.

Colleen studied and went to school around the clock. She would leave around six o'clock every morning to catch the bus and return around six to eight o'clock in the evening. Almost every day Colleen had a quiz that had to be completed before midnight or get a big, fat zero. She also had lesson plans and other work she needed to read for the next day. I tried to help her study. Most of the time, I found myself so tired that I went to bed between eleven p.m. and midnight. Colleen would still be studying long after I went to bed. She persevered despite the long, sleepless nights. I know it was the Lord holding her up. I knew the Lord would be with her despite the punishing schedule. I prayed for her a lot.

After about two weeks, I noticed Colleen seemed to feel the end was in sight. She had more of a bounce in her step. Things did not seem to be as difficult. With renewed confidence, she powered her way through the rest of the course. Shortly before graduation, I visited her school and took flowers to her to celebrate our anniversary. I was so proud of her. She completed the course in one month and had prevailed. I saw God at work in her and it taught me a lot about perseverance.

Speaking of perseverance, on Thanksgiving Day in 2016, a hurricane struck the northern part of Costa Rica. We were enjoying an American traditional Thanksgiving meal with all the trimmings. Costa Ricans were learning about Thanksgiving because of the United States' influence. I was thankful for the wonderful meal and fellowship. However, sadness was in the air.

We knew that a hurricane was hitting the north. We were praying and hoping that it would turn or somehow miss Costa Rica. We soon learned that Hurricane Otto struck northern Costa Rica and killed nine people. Officials reported rainfall of close to a month's worth in several hours.

Upala was an area hit especially hard. Colleen and I, as well as our community, had connections with a church in Upala. We had completed an outreach with the team earlier in the year with a church from that area. Some of the staff from VidaNet had family in Upala.

The missionary school sent a team to help with the cleanup effort and provide support as needed. As well, there was a generous community response from all of Costa Rica to help.

Driving to Upala, we saw firsthand the devastation. Huge boulders and cars had been tossed around like rag dolls. Some houses were destroyed. Trees and power lines were down throughout the area. The rain had pushed mountains of mud everywhere. Almost all the houses in the Upala area were filled with about one to two feet of mud. Most people in that area lost all their possessions.

We helped with cleaning the mud out of one house. It took

eight staff members all day long to clear out most of the mud from that one house. At first, it seemed like an overwhelming and impossible task. With all the mud, we did not know what we were going to find. The mud was so deep that it nearly sucked my boots off. Just one house took so long to clean up. There were many more houses just like it. Until you see a disaster in person, you will never understand how it affects people. You will never understand the gravity of the situation. It pales in comparison to seeing it on TV.

There was an outpouring of manpower and needed items to begin the recovery process. Even though there were losses, God gave in abundance to provide hope for those who desperately needed it. It was the community of Costa Rica that saw the need and responded in love with action. Some of the team members made several more trips to that area to continue with the relief effort. Many prayers were offered for strength and perseverance. There was still a lot of work to be done, but hope was on the way.

There were many more things that happened in Costa Rica. Too many to mention. The main thing that caught our attention was that God loved us first, and because of that, we wanted to love Him.

As a result of this, we started to love people in a different way. The wonderful thing was that it all seemed to be happening in community. Even our marriage was changing. We were starting to work more as a community. I did seem to be a couple of steps behind, but I was gaining ground instead of losing ground. It was all done in community. Community. Community. Community. I hope you are seeing a theme here.

Leaving Costa Rica was not easy. We had lived in community for one year. We were ministering to others in community. We were connecting with churches to build and strengthen community. We had lived in Costa Rica long enough that we became accustomed to the lifestyle. We had developed such great relationships. We established many relationships with a variety of people. We even took in a twenty-three-year-old roommate and referred to her as our adopted daughter. She lived with us for most of the year. We became quite close with her as well as many others. Even our landlord sang a Spanish song to us before we left; it brought us to tears. It was hard to leave.

We had struggled with the language, but we had been there long enough that we could communicate to get by. Studying the language helped us to connect so that we were becoming a part of the culture. Learning the language was exceedingly difficult but speaking it seemed to be more difficult. I began to understand as a foreigner, how difficult it was to live in a culture where language was a barrier. However, most people were willing to overlook our poor Spanish. Some Costa Ricans spoke English, or knew enough, so it was not a total wash.

Learning Spanish was just one of the many transitions. We had been a part of the transition from the old base for VidaNet, referring to it as "tent city." The old base consisted of several large tents and makeshift structures. The new base was a monumental step up as far as accommodations. The new base was permanent and could accommodate growth. It had enormous potential. Many years of prayer had preceded that transition. We helped move many of the items from the old base to the new one as one of our last projects. Each day, we would take several van loads to the new base. It took several weeks but the team was finally able to clear out the old base. We also helped with cleaning the new base as well as painting many of the rooms. Colleen said she often felt like she had painted half of Costa Rica.

We felt grateful and thankful just to be a part of that process. Something that was finally coming together because of a vision. We were just beginning to feel comfortable in a totally new environment and now our time was up. We struggled with whether we should stay and continue ministering in Costa Rica. We felt that we were more equipped; but for what? There was an opportunity to stay and further disciple those students who had completed the missionary training school. We saw discipleship, ESL, and community as part of the bigger picture. Again, no particular people group came to our minds. We still had questions as usual. My mind drifted back to Clarkston. For some reason, I could not quite get Clarkston out of my mind.

Our last days in Costa Rica were extremely tough. It seemed as if everyone in Costa Rica wanted to throw us a party. The VidaNet mission, our landlord, and the church we attended all had parties to send us off. The list went on and on. Several of the church members made homemade gifts for us to take home as mementos. We were certainly blessed beyond measure. As we attended each party, it became more difficult.

We had to fight our feelings. We did not want to stay in Costa Rica based on feelings. We wanted to honor God and follow His lead, not just do something because it looked good or because it fits with our skills or training. We knew we had to be faithful and take the next step. We wanted to hear from God, and off to the United States we headed again.

11

Moving at the Speed of Light

As soon as we hit the airport in Columbus, Ohio, I had an overwhelming feeling that our lives were going to be busier than ever. Our sons had planned their weddings within a week of each other. Their thinking seemed to be that they better catch Mom and Dad while they could. They were never sure where we might end up. Colleen and I were not even sure ourselves.

Coming back to the States was a huge adjustment. Talk about reverse culture shock. We had been moving at a snail's pace as a lifestyle, which we came to enjoy; now we were moving at the speed of light. I cannot emphasize enough how dramatic that change was. For the next two weeks, we helped with planning our two sons' weddings. It was a big moment for both. We were simply happy to celebrate with them and to help as needed. We loved our sons and wanted the best for them.

It was good to see them step into that role. We continue to pray for them in this area. God uses a married couple in Christ to show His glory and His image. Marriage is meant to be an image of our relationship with Christ. It is to be an image that should reflect God's glory and righteousness. I believe this is the reason why the family unit and marriage are being attacked today. Mankind, as an image-bearer, is important to God as we were made to reflect His image. My hope is that our sons and our daughters-in-law will catch that vision of what a marriage represents. We pray that they will love and serve one another out of their love and devotion to God.

As we moved forward after the weddings, we were still in reverse-culture-shock mode. Huge retail stores were even more disconcerting. I am amazed at the options that the US provides. Aisle after aisle of cereals, toothpastes, drinks, and the like. Just about anything you can imagine is at your fingertips. It just engulfed us. I often felt so overwhelmed by all the options. I have trouble even finding basic items due to all the options that are available. Options can be good, but Henry Ford had it right. His idea was to make a car that is black, and all the options are the same. I know that sounds boring, but sometimes even boring can be okay.

As far as the pace of life in general, we felt off-balance. Everything seemed so hectic. Everything seemed to move faster in the United States. Even though the traffic was insane in Costa Rica at times, it is on a much slower schedule than in the States. In Costa Rica, the top speed limit on a few of the open roads was around 105 kilometers per hour (65 miles an hour.) In most places outside the city, it was 72 to 88 kilometers per hour (45 to 55 miles per hour.) Everything seemed so rushed in the US—go here, go there. Schedules were crammed with stuff to do. Resting in the Lord was much harder to do. In Costa Rica, we had become accustomed to taking an hour of quiet time each day to hear the Lord. We also had a devotion after that. "No rest for the weary" was our new motto. Everyone else's schedule was also busy, and it became harder to connect. Harder to feel like a part of a community. We felt out of sorts.

Overwhelmed or not, we had a decision to make; much prayer was needed. Things did not slow down, but God put on my heart to explore Clarkston, Georgia, again to see what other opportunities might be available for ministry. We made several trips to Clarkston throughout the summer and autumn seasons, staying about a month at a time. I wanted to visit Clarkston to scout the area and look at all the available options.

On our first trip to Georgia, we received bad news. One of our close friends from Costa Rica had suddenly died from a heart problem. It was hard to understand her death. She had meant so much to us and was a vital part of the VidaNet staff in Costa Rica. She was a friend to all in Christ. We prayed a lot and wept bitterly. We prayed for strength and perseverance for the VidaNet family as our friend would be truly missed. We were grieving but we had to stay focused on the task at hand. We connected with GFM and some other agencies to see their ministries in action.

On another one of our trips to Clarkston, we had further contact with GFM. We met with one of the GFM staff, the same staff member I met during the Harvest Week in 2015. He indicated that GFM wanted to start a discipleship team that would focus on evangelism, the discipleship process, possibly ESL, and working with internationals. That word—"internationals"—caught my attention. His vision of discipleship seemed to fit with our vision. When we traveled back to Ohio, it hit me. We had not found a particular people group to minister to. Connecting with internationals seemed to be a way of possibly reaching the nations.

It was all coming together. It would be done in community as a team. Over the next several months, GFM staff introduced us to a process called "No Place Left" as a way of making disciples. A coalition of believers formed that wanted to reach others with the Gospel and train new followers to become disciples. Not only that but this process also looked at how disciples would make more disciples. "Disciples who want to make disciples who want to make more disciples." *Want* is the key word. Our team would be looking for those who wanted to make disciples. Multiplication was a key ingredient.

We investigated this process further and found it to be biblical and reproducing. This whole process was nothing new. One of the things that caught our attention was the simplicity of the trainings. A reproducible process is important so that things can be easily learned and easily passed on to others. The materials helped us to discover who to go to and what to say when sharing the Gospel. We looked at building up disciples and how to form communities of believers. We would also discover how to develop leaders with their God-given spiritual abilities to maintain the discipleship process. This would encourage and help maintain a multiplication movement.

We formed a team to continue looking at the materials and to process the information. I was very keen on the process of working as a team. It was a lot of material, so we had a lot to process and think through. As we studied the material throughout the summer, it appeared that we were headed in the right direction. There was still a lot of prayer needed and bugs to be worked out. We all were interested in the team process and began to discuss what that might look like with each of us using our God-given talents. As we continued to meet, we were getting to know each other better and we were developing a strong sense of community.

We spoke to Globe International (our missionary sponsoring agency) and they wanted to endorse the process of No Place Left and the idea of partnering with GFM. After much prayer and confirmation about the international connections, we decided to go to Clarkston to be trained in the No Place Left process. We again talked with Globe International and they fully endorsed us to be "loaned" to GFM to form a partnership. Globe was interested in the Clarkston/Atlanta area and saw it as a possible training ground, maybe even a hub, a pipeline to the nations. As well, we had been involved in an unreached people group initiative with Globe. Globe was excited about the prospect that we might engage certain unreached people groups that are in the Clarkston/Atlanta area.

It was exciting to see that God was using Clarkston and other areas of the country because of their diversity. Our plan was to attend several intensive trainings of the No Place Left process. Our eventual goal would be to disciple others by training them with this same approach.

In January 2018, we packed our bags and headed for Clarkston, Georgia. Again, Colleen struggled with leaving her mother, our children, and my dad. Our parents were getting older and had started to develop some health problems. Driving from Georgia to Ohio on a regular basis was not always an option. Colleen had forged a strong bond with her family, and it was quite difficult for her to give that up. Again, we had to admit that God was bigger than our separation from our family and that He was totally capable of taking care of our family. We, in fact, had a job to do. I knew God was up to something in Clarkston and He was calling us to be a part of it.

When we arrived, we did not have a permanent place to live, so we stayed with some friends for one month. We had connected with them from our previous scouting trips. Slowing down just did not seem to be an option. Immediately, we completed our first five-day intensive training in January 2018. *Intense* is an understatement. We had studied the material all through the summer and fall before going to Georgia, so it was not new information. However, there were still key concepts that we just did not catch yet. We still had not connected all the dots.

We wanted to develop what we were teaching as a lifestyle. We did not want to just learn material. We wanted to put it into practice. Most of what we had studied would be crammed into a five-day training. It made for long days. A lot of information was packed into those five days. Even though the training sessions were jam-packed, we started to see a vision of how we might train and incorporate these basic principles. The basic process shows how a person is led from lostness to leadership; it is called the Four Fields Kingdom Growth Process. Once a person is called into the Kingdom of God by repenting and accepting, through faith, Jesus's death, burial, and resurrection from the dead, they will want to naturally love God and serve others because of His great love. A process can be initiated to help disciples to know where to go, what to say, how Christ can build up and strengthen them as well as other disciples, how to gather disciples together in community, and how to develop leaders who will want to continue this process.

As followers of Christ, we understand that this is not the only way to do discipleship. There are many methods. Methods are not the goal; they are only a means. The goal is to show people Christ.

God is to be glorified through what Christ is doing in us and others. One of the main things to realize is that God is the one who regenerates life and causes growth. God is the one that saves through faith and trust in Jesus Christ. We are merely participants in that plan working out. This key concept cannot be overlooked. God is the one who causes growth and changes the hearts of people.

Our month was almost up, and we still had not found a place to live. Due to our original agreement, we could only stay one month and needed to move out. I was at a prayer meeting with some GFM staff and others and I mentioned our housing dilemma as a prayer concern. At the end of the prayer, a six-foot, six-inch gentleman stood up; he had been doing ministry in the Clarkston/Stone Mountain area with his wife. He mentioned that maybe we could stay with him and his wife. I was surprised as I did not know him from Adam. I talked with him a few more times over the phone. His wife approved, and before we knew it, we were moving in with them.

It was God's providence right away. It just so happened that our newfound friends had worked with a friend of ours from Columbus, Ohio. Prior to coming to Clarkston, we had met with this friend in Columbus. He briefly mentioned that he knew a couple in Clarkston and had worked with them on the field as team leaders. He did not mention their names specifically. This was the very same couple whom we had moved in with. Small world.

There was a connection right away. This couple let us stay with them for six months and we became exceptionally close friends. I listened to my newfound friend as he discussed his many years serving in ministry. He ministered to people from the Middle East. He loved people in general and had a heart for prayer. It was incredible to know that we were not alone. His story and mine were extremely similar. We had a lot in common (except for his height). We were about the same age, so we were experiencing many of the same life issues. Colleen seemed to have a lot in common with his wife as well. I felt so blessed to be surrounded by people who had such wisdom and experience. I was a learner all over again. My friend eventually joined our training team and added depth to what we were teaching.

We attended two more intensive trainings just to get a good handle on the teachings. Again, this made for long days, but our investment started to pay dividends. We seemed to finally catch the bigger picture and were connecting a lot more dots. We still had questions and more dots to connect, but we felt confident that we could start training other believers. We had confidence in God that He would be with us to move us forward even if we did not have all the details. In our teachings, we say that we love "FAT people"—those people who are Faithful, Available, and Teachable. These three characteristics will propel people to act. Now it was time to put into practice what we had learned.

I remember one of our first trainings: Our team helped coach an African American-Caribbean church. The pastor of that church had gone through the initial intensive training with us. He wanted to train his church but needed a team to help him. We trained for part of a day and then went to a motel to do outreach. We all ministered to the people at the motel. We had several fruitful contacts. What we did not know was that God had already planted a person of peace before we arrived.

The pastor went into the main office to talk with the manager of the motel. As the pastor discussed with the manager what he was doing, the manager became intrigued. He asked the pastor to come back and further discuss his ideas; the manager liked what he saw. Talk about a person of peace. We had nothing to do with that except be available. This manager could now be influenced as he was open to the messenger, the message, and the mission. His relational map (people that he knew) was off the chart as he had influence with most of the people at the motel.

This pastor shared his vision with his congregation. His vision was met with enthusiasm by some, but others were resistant. So resistant that they left his church. We grieved with him over his loss, but he did press forward. Having a vision for discipleship is God's heart, but there is a cost. Grace was free to all, but our dear

Lord and Savior paid the ultimate cost for that freedom. This same pastor later lost his son in a tragic shooting.

His testimony was powerful about how he had no malice toward the man that took his son's life. He only wanted to respond in peace and honor the Lord Jesus. I grieved for his loss and prayed for him. I simply made myself available to help him in any way I could. We were thankful for those who pressed forward despite the obstacles faced. We were thankful for helping us encounter those who saw the importance of living a life for Christ despite the costs.

Time and time again, our team would pray for the right church or people to train to further advance the Kingdom of God. To connect with people who were hungry for the Word and things of God. We were also hoping to connect with others who would want to follow Christ's example and be disciples. Not only be disciples but be disciple-makers. We were also looking for leaders who exemplified what we call "fourth soil" persons from the Parable of the Sower and the Soil (Mark 4:1–9). Those people who want to go deep into the Word to produce an increase of thirty-fold, sixty-fold, and on-hundred-fold.

We had connected with several other churches as well. Our team leader had connected with a Baptist church prior to our arrival. Our team leader and his wife had been working with that Baptist church for about a year before our arrival. Colleen and I started where our leaders left off. We helped this church by just being available and continuing to reinforce some of the No Place Left trainings as well as attending outreaches in two nearby communities. We were available to model prayer walking and sharing our faith. Prayer walking is a way to connect with God and observe what is going on around you. Prayer walking helps depend on God to open doors to His work. One of the ladies of this church already had a heart to meet others and see people come to Christ. All we did was encourage her to keep pressing forward.

At times she felt discouraged because of the lack of participation from her church.

One Saturday, no one came for outreach. Colleen and I prayed with her that God would do something, and people might catch the vision to go out and share their faith. No sooner had we finished praying and a car pulled up. A man with his children had heard that we were going out on outreach today. He wanted to be a part of the outreach team. He shared his testimony with us, and it was enormously powerful. He had been delivered from alcohol and other issues, and he felt a calling to go out and share his faith. God continued to amaze us. Just when we thought that all hope was lost, He came to the rescue.

God continued to open doors with other churches as well. Our team did a training session at a Vietnamese church's youth gathering. We did a training about identity in Christ and how to share the Gospel using the "3-Circles Gospel Share." The 3-Circles Gospel Share is a simple tool to effectively share God's story about how He reconciled a broken relationship with mankind to himself. We looked at the idea of becoming a new creation and how we have been called to be Christ's ambassador (2 Corinthians 5:17–21). Seven kids were saved by Christ that night.

Our intention was to train the youth and the leaders to help them along with their journey toward discipleship. We gave them tools to help with evangelism, but God did so much more. We cried and wept as it was very emotional. I discovered that the Vietnamese church youth leaders had been pouring into the kids for years. They had plowed the ground so that the seed could eventually grow. The team just added some water and fertilizer.

We continued to follow up with them throughout the summer. The youth and its leaders were strengthened and encouraged. Time and time again, I began to realize that whatever God was doing had already been set up by much prayer beforehand.

12

Living Communities

Prayer is vitally important in connecting with God to worship Him and make our requests known to Him. Prayer had been offered by the saints (believers in Christ) sometimes years before the prayers were fully answered.

I began meeting with three to four prayer partners on a regular basis. I noticed that my prayer partners were praying for a house gathering in each of the apartment complexes in Clarkston. As our team began to teach No Place Left processes to leaders, pastors, churches, and others, we noticed that small gatherings were popping up in several of the apartment complexes in Clarkston. I found out that these prayer partners had been praying about this for about three years before I had arrived in Clarkston. God was moving because the faithful were willing to commit time in prayer and ask the Father. Again and again, it was committed and extensive prayer that preceded God's moving. These gentlemen would not only be my prayer partners but would become good friends that I could count on. Friends that would be there for me when I needed them and vice versa.

As I continue in ministry, I am convinced that any work that is done in Christ's name was set up by prayer. The examples that I have personally seen with this are too numerous to list. When something happens, I am always looking for how the groundwork was laid beforehand. People just do not show up and things happen; the works of God are related to prayer, the Word, the

Holy Spirit, community, and looking for His timing. Prayer helped us build community and depend on God to move us toward being living communities—communities that were becoming more like Christ and were active because of faith.

Colleen and I began to feel the need to get our own place. Things were beginning to slow down a little and we wanted to settle into the Clarkston area on a more permanent basis. We prayed about this. We had lived in Stone Mountain for six months. It was wonderful getting to know our dear friends who had helped us so much. They were at a place where their family and ministry needs were changing, hence the need for us to move on.

We were able to connect with a strong leader who had been in Clarkston for many years. She was a missionary who loved people and especially liked to help other missionaries. She had a place for rent in her basement and wanted us to check it out. After prayerful consideration, we agreed to sign a lease for a year.

Packing the rest of our stuff from Ohio, we moved into her basement and officially became residents of Clarkston, Georgia. It was a good move for us. The Lord had provided so many wonderful connections for us so far and we knew that He would continue to do so. Our new landlord was well connected with the community of Clarkston and knew just about everyone in ministry. She also knew the local resources. She started the Friends of Refugees (FOR) in the 1990s which was a mainstay organization for helping refugees in the Clarkston area. She was no longer in the administration of the FOR, but she was still strongly connected with them. If we had a question or needed help finding resources, we could always turn to her. Over the years, she had developed a strong network of connections. We called her "the Guru of Clarkston."

She had such wonderful stories and we could tell she loved God and people. She had such a heart for helping missionaries. We felt so honored and blessed to know her. She often said that if you lived in her house, you were her family; we certainly felt like family, like a small community.

As we were like a family, we depended on each other. We helped each other and looked out for one another; it was much more than a landlord and tenant relationship. Due to her connections and generosity, she had developed a lot of family over the years. As well, she had rented out her basement to many people. She was a person of peace. For her, community was everything. She enjoyed being around others and helping wherever she could. We would include her in some of our trainings with Globe International as she could tell the story of Clarkston's history so well. She also had numerous stories about her involvement with FOR. I often watched the others as she told stories of Clarkston and her connections with others. Her sweet disposition and soft voice captured their imagination. Again and again, God was putting people in our path who had experience as missionaries or who had access to resources through networking.

We were becoming blessed with the community aspect more than ever. As we continue to meet different people in communities, we have been able to contribute and build strong bonds that last a lifetime. Personally, this has been one of the most rewarding aspects of being on mission with God. I have developed key relationships that have shown me the complexity and diversity of God. These relationships often kept me going because it was one of the ways God encouraged me and helped me to be faithful. I have been privileged and honored to meet so many people that have enriched my life and helped me grow in the knowledge and grace of our Lord Jesus Christ. It has truly been an adventure of a lifetime.

One of the things that still seemed to elude me was that idea of soccer and how it could relate to ministry. The question would come up from time to time. How did soccer fit in all this, and how could it be a type of ministry? I had no clue. I needed guidance so I kept asking. Little did I know how important my connection with soccer would become. It would indeed develop into a living community.

One day, I was at a prayer meeting and one of the GFM staff

members mentioned that he was taking some boys to soccer. This obviously caught my attention. He explained that he was involved with the Fellowship of Christian Athletes (FCA) and helped twice a week coaching the Clarkston soccer team. He said he started out not knowing a lot about soccer but enjoyed it and the connections it provided. Sounds familiar. I asked him more about it and planned to get together with him. Could this be it? Could this be the connection that I was looking for?

I prayed about it. I discussed this potential opportunity with my prayer partners and they immediately prayed for clarity and that God would open the door if I needed to pursue FCA as an option.

Shortly after that prayer meeting, I attended another prayer meeting regarding unreached people groups in the Atlanta/Clarkston area. At that prayer meeting, I met a man who served in a soccer ministry in the Atlanta area. I had never met him before. Again, my senses were heightened. When we each discussed our specific ministry and prayer concerns, he mentioned his ministry was working with FCA. My curiosity was at an all-time high.

After the prayer meeting, I asked him about his connection with FCA. It was not a coincidence that he was the leader of the FCA in the Atlanta area. Not only was he the leader of FCA but he had been a professional player for seven years and was also the chaplain for a professional soccer team in Atlanta. Talk about connections. I discussed my interest in soccer as a ministry and set up a meeting with him.

I still had no clue how this would work out, but for the first time, I felt encouraged that there might be an avenue to use soccer as a ministry. We met and he discussed his vision and how I might be a part of that. Shortly afterward, he decided to have me be a part of his team as a volunteer.

As I continued to pray, it was evident that moving forward in faith and starting to partner with FCA was the thing to do. I began connecting with the Clarkston team about halfway through the soccer season. I was surrounded by talented coaches and some neat kids. It was amazing to see the passion these coaches had for soccer and sharing Christ with the kids.

During practices, we shared life lessons from Bible stories. On game day, we would discuss the life lesson and how it went that week. We were sharing the Gospel with little or no pushback.

As far as the actual soccer end of it, it was quite evident that I needed a lot of work on my soccer skills. With no formal training, my soccer skills were practically nonexistent. I was pretty much starting from ground zero skill-wise. I learned so much about positioning, different drills, and skills that had to be developed. I was so blessed to be around guys who were talented at soccer.

Despite my physical limitations, I continued to press on. All the coaches loved the kids and showed Christ to them. We all wanted the kids to work hard and apply themselves. We also wanted them to know there was much more to life than soccer. I was a learner all over again.

We worked with two teams—one was U-13 and the other U-16. My lack of knowledge and skill was very apparent as some of the U-13 were good enough, they should have been coaching me. It was okay; I was a learner. They seemed to know that I wanted to learn and be available as needed. We practiced once a week and had games on Saturdays. The season ended with the U-13 doing well in the tournament but losing in the finals. The U-16 team reached the finals and won the tournament. It was an exciting season. It was wonderful to see the kids work so hard and be successful on and off the field.

The next season rolled around, and I was ready to go again. This time, I was a coach; that took some getting used to. I still had a lot to learn and, due to my age, seemed to be a step behind physically. The coaches and players gave me plenty of grace. I certainly needed it. I was willing to keep learning and be a part of their lives.

All the coaches poured into the kids all season long. There were many lessons to learn. At the end of the day, the U-16 won the tournament again and the U-13 lost a hard-fought battle in the finals. During the season, I was invited to go with the kids to a professional soccer game in Atlanta. I know it was special for them. It was a big deal for me as well. We were working on doing more than just soccer together. We were beginning to live life-on-life.

Gearing up for the next season, FCA hosted a summer camp, which I was a part of. It was fun and the Great Commission was discussed during the week. Jesus called his disciples in the Great Commission to go and make disciples of all nations, baptizing them and teaching them to obey everything He had commanded them. At the end of the commission, Jesus promised that He would be with his disciples always, even to the end of the age.

The kids studied the Great Commission step by step, and what it meant to be a disciple. The kids were learning how a disciple is to live out his life. The kids were learning how to connect with Jesus, and they were also honing their soccer skills.

A short-term team joined the summer camp and provided some additional coaches. Some of the coaches were incredibly experienced and talented, which added depth to the training. It was truly a community effort. I finished the camp and started to attend regular weekly practices. The coaching staff formed our teams for the autumn season.

The coaching staff decided to add U-19 to the schedule. We were now working with three teams. We were fortunate to have enough coaches who were flexible to cover the three teams. What a blessing. I also attended a training that looked at methods and techniques to help with mentoring youth. One of the keys to coaching is the ability to impact the athletes' hearts as well as teach them soccer skills. Winning matters, but it is not the main objective. Winning is an outcome of coaching the heart of the athlete. Long-lasting impact comes from the ability to influence and to develop an athlete who becomes an agent of change over their lifespan.

As the season progressed, there were several issues that needed to be addressed regarding behavior. The coaches were firm with their discipline but also showed grace. The coaches were encouraged because of the way the kids carried themselves at the games. The kids were very respectful to the referees and other coaches. They were notable examples of how to conduct themselves when others were not good examples. As coaches, we worked with them to build team skills and character. We had a few kids who stood out because of their excellent soccer skills. We encouraged them as leaders so the whole team could benefit.

By the end of the year, their hard work paid off. The U-19 won the championship and played one of their best games of the year. The U-16 lost three to two in the first round of the tournament. The U-13 reached the finals for the third year in a row (the previous two years they were runners-up). It was another hard-fought battle, and the game went into overtime. Each team had five penalty kicks and our goalie made a great save on the last kick. This year, they prevailed and won the championship. The team and coaches learned about perseverance. After the victory, each one of the kids surrounded each coach and prayed for them, it was a special moment for all involved.

What an amazing season. We had learned, laughed, cried, and became a family together. We were becoming a living community!

13

More to Come

U sing soccer was a way to easily break down ministry barriers but there was one barrier that seemed to be more difficult than others. Due to the number of languages and dialects in Clarkston and surrounding areas, it is quite difficult to have spiritual conversations with some people. Sometimes in Clarkston, we would meet people and their only response was, "No English."

One day, we were ministering in the community with a Christian brother from Nepal. We were talking with an Afghani lady, and it was difficult to communicate due to the language barrier. It was hard to even get a conversation started. Suddenly, our friend started talking to her. I had no idea he could speak four languages. What a gift from God! Our team and GFM had been praying about this as the language barrier seemed almost too difficult to overcome. Learning all the languages in the area would be impossible.

Our friend was able to connect with the Afghani lady when we were unable to communicate. We had a few interpreters before, but something made me think about how our believing brothers and sisters from other ethnicities could more effectively share the Gospel in the Clarkston area and beyond. After praying, we started to use the relational map idea. What if we could find believers who spoke English and spoke several other languages? We could train them and teach them some easy tools about where to go, what to share, how to build disciples, how to gather disciples, and how to form leaders.

It was unbelievable how we were able to train believers who already had a heart for being on missions with God and desired to share God's Word. They also had language and culture, which enabled them to connect in ways that we could not.

Our team trained at a Nepali church. After the training, their pastor took what he had learned from No Place Left and trained many churches all over the country. He was excited about the training and opportunities to share his faith and build up disciples. He went to Ohio, Minnesota, New York, and even to the nations abroad to do trainings in other Nepali churches. Before leaving on a mission trip, he contacted people in Asia by phone and trained them. He was preparing them beforehand. Some of those trained over the phone did outreach and shared the Gospel before he even arrived. These believers were trained further, and they would share the Gospel not only in their country but also with other nations. Brothers and sisters from other ethnicities who had come to the US were now going back to their homelands or connecting in other ways. They were sharing with the nations; some were sharing with the unreached.

Another pastor that went through the Clarkston Bible Institute (CBI) was trained by our team in the No Place Left process. He wanted to go back to the Ivory Coast and train his church so they could be more mission-minded and go out with the Gospel. To further prepare for his return, he joined the staff at Clarkston Bible Institute to hone his teaching skills. He also joined our training team to do a three-day intensive training at CBI.

Our team also trained some Sudanese pastors and leaders. The day before the training, I had given up all hope that the training would even happen. Our team leader received several calls at the last minute and the training would miraculously happen as planned. The training went well, and the Sudanese were so appreciative of our help. They felt more equipped to reach Sudan.

The leaders and pastors mentioned that Sudan was open more than ever due to a change in leadership in their country. We later found out that there had been a revolution in Sudan that dramatically changed the landscape. After the training, I wept because I was convinced that the training would not happen. I had given up all hope that it would go off as planned. I even doubted God. I repented from my unwillingness to hear God when He was at work doing something. It was incredible how God worked it out despite my lack of faith. God came through and saw that the Sudanese people would be encouraged and that it was His timing, not mine.

Through the trainings, we were finding people who had unbelievable relational maps. These believers in the Clarkston/Atlanta area were moving beyond their close personal spheres of influence and moving toward influencing the world.

The No Place Left process has good material, but it is just the beginning of things to come. It is not the only method or process for developing discipleship and obeying the Great Commission. We have had to restructure and tweak our trainings many times over. The training looks quite a bit different than our first few times. We had to simplify the teachings so that they represented cultural and language differences. We moved more toward training others to be trainers themselves. The basic principles were the same without all the fluff.

We were finding people who had a heart for God and had unbelievable connections within their own personal sphere of influence. Many of these leaders and pastors had trained and disciplined others for years in their own countries. Some just needed a few more simple tools for their toolbox. Their faith was so deep and genuine. Others reported that they now had a more strategic way to share the Gospel. They felt more confident and empowered to start conversations and share God's Word. They genuinely wanted to reach their own culture as well as other cultures.

One such man was from the Congo. His testimony was incredible. He fled the Congo and stayed in Uganda for eighteen years. While in Uganda, he traveled on his motorcycle from place to place and set up a film about Jesus. The film about Jesus accurately portrays the life of Jesus as depicted in the book of Luke.

Hundreds of people came and watched the film and many professed Christ as their Lord and Savior. Over those eighteen years, he had personally seen the film about Jesus so many times in other languages, that he added five new languages to his existing two languages. Simply amazing.

His entire family of twelve ended up in Clarkston after being separated, poisoned, and threatened with death in Uganda. When his last son finally arrived in Clarkston, many participated in a gathering to celebrate their reunion. Despite the hardships his family faced, they were all together. It was truly a miracle as it is extremely unusual to have all a refugee family relocate to the same area, especially with such a large family. This was truly a man of God, and he knew how to bring believers together in worship, prayer, and studying God's Word. His family had come to America to start a Swahili/English church.

We trained some of them with some basic Gospel-sharing tools and a few other tools to develop discipleship. We were glad to connect with the Swahili/English gathering. As far as training, we did not need to do much. This man had been planting churches and making disciples for most of his life. He had at least six certificates and a degree from his many years of studying the Word. Ministry came naturally to him. He was certainly a man of peace. He would say, after meeting a person once, that they were now a part of the church. His house was theirs and they were no longer a stranger but now a friend. He embodied the principle of a person of peace.

Even more, his whole lifestyle was about peace and grace. He described how, in Africa, the Christian community demonstrated peace. In some African cultures, when there is a death in a family, the whole community gets involved to help those grieving. The community comes together in peace and compassion to lighten the load of the family members who suffered a loss. The whole community benefited by banding together in solidarity. They suffered together in unity, and it helped to strengthen the community.

As Colleen and I continued to attend this Swahili/English

church gathering in Clarkston, we were strengthened as well. There were many healings that took place. Some in the community were drawn to this gathering due to hearing about these miracles. They were also coming because they had heard about a message of peace. This is what a gathering should look like. Each person has gifts the Holy Spirit gives; each person participates in building up the body; each member has a function. There was such love and devotion to one another, we were glad to be a part of such a gathering. The Bible says to love one another. By loving one another, we show the love of Christ to outsiders. Our love for one another draws people to the Gospel message. Our love for one another also strengthens the entire body and encourages each other to be faithful and keep pressing on.

There was an evangelist in this same body of Swahili/English believers. Some of us started going out with this evangelist on outreach. We would knock on doors and look for other people of peace. We were making connections with others again and people were using their gifts. People were responding to healings and there were some who responded to the Gospel.

On one outreach, this evangelist and I shared with a man from Iraq. Both of us shared our testimony and he seemed engaged, but somehow, we were not quite connecting. I asked the man from Iraq if he had any visions or dreams. He told us that he had three dreams about a man who was all white and there was no darkness in him. He seemed almost apologetic as, somehow, he felt we did not believe him. We immediately sensed Jesus was trying to reveal himself to the Iraqi man. We pointed out to him that the man in white in his dreams was indeed Jesus. We were certain that God was directly trying to show himself.

As we continued to talk, we realized, due to the language barrier, that we still were not quite connecting. We certainly needed help in making a deeper connection. My friend, the evangelist, decided to download the Bible to his phone in his language. As the Iraqi man read from the first chapter of John, his eyes lit up. He had never read anything like it. I could tell he was deep in thought and was utterly amazed. He seemed to make the connection that the Jesus he had been dreaming about was indeed in the Bible.

We prayed with him, and he seemed so happy. Multiple follow-ups were planned with him but, for whatever reason, we only connected on the surface. He reported he was reading the Bible but with the language barrier, it was difficult to figure out what he was actually learning. Colleen and I also tried to connect him with a strong Iraqi believer but that also did not materialize. We proceeded to pray for him, as connecting further was not working out. We continued to hope and pray that the good work the Lord had started would somehow continue.

As this Swahili/English gathering kept growing, we prayed about the next step. As a result of growth, another gathering started. The gathering now met in a rent-free facility and had plenty of space for more growth. Praise be to the Father. Healthy churches were producing growth.

This Congolese brother who started this house church soon felt a calling to move on. It was hard to see him go but we knew he had been called elsewhere. This Congolese brother ended up connecting with others in Ohio to serve in ministry and pass on the message of peace and salvation. He plans to do the same thing in Ohio that he did in Clarkston. He will use his gift of peace to plant gatherings and minister to others. Our part was to continue praying for him. Also, we wanted to continue to be faithful, available, and teachable in being that person of peace for others. By faith, we moved forward knowing it is not in our own strength or might; the battle is the Lord's. God is good and He knows what is best for us, even if we do not always know the why or all the next steps.

As well as our regular house gathering, Colleen and I were able to attend church at the Atlanta Vineyard in Brookhaven, Georgia. Colleen and I were accepted as family. We felt a sense of belonging that was incredible. The Vineyard church had an outreach at a motel, and they had been ministering there for the past five years.

Part of the ministry included a Bible study for the residents of the motel. I started to attend this weekly Bible study. I never knew who was going to show up and need the Gospel, a word, or a simple act of kindness. It was incredible to attend outreach at the motel and pray for many. The Vineyard continued further outreach once a month at the motel by passing out toiletries and other basic hygiene items. We divided into teams to minister and pray for the residents of the motel. The church also had a cookout at the motel once a month.

Throughout this process, several people at the motel have responded to the Gospel. They had put their faith and trust in other things, sometimes in people. They had been let down by others and some even felt God had let them down. They were hurt and wounded, but once they caught the idea that they could trust Jesus, it made all the difference in the world. We were also able to encourage many believers who had fallen on hard times. Staying at the motel was difficult and many were losing hope. They just needed encouragement and a helping hand. As the body of Christ, we were responding with action in love to those who were in need.

I was also able to be part of a men's Bible study, mainly comprised of several internationals. I have learned so much from them. I learned a lot from their respective cultures. Their depth and study of the Word were incredible. Prayer was of the utmost importance and concern. These men have encouraged me and strengthened my faith by fellowshipping together as a community of believers. Studying the Word encouraged us to obey so that we were putting into practice what we had heard.

Another believer invited me to go to downtown Atlanta and help with a homeless ministry. We prayed for many and handed out food. Many responded positively and a few committed their lives to Christ. Some were negative and did not want anything to do with us. Some claimed to be believers but continued to live a life in sin. They were claiming that Jesus had changed them but were unwilling to give up their sin. It was challenging at times, but we shared and prayed with those who were willing to listen. We also continued to pray for those who had rejected Jesus or were not interested.

Again, working with believers in the community was a way to show the love of Christ in a tangible way. I cannot put into words how God has been faithful to do these things; it is God and God alone, with the power of the Holy Spirit and the blood of the Lamb that makes all the difference. Again, we just had to be faithful, available, and teachable to move to the next step.

14

Reaching Abroad by Training Nationals

R eaching the nations abroad has been something that has been on our hearts. We did see the benefit of working in Clarkston but, from time to time, there seemed to be a tug on our hearts to go to other nations. We were hoping that we could train believers in the Clarkston/Atlanta area and abroad to strengthen and encourage them to share not only with people that they knew but also outside of their own personal influence. The trainings were important, but God wanted more.

Colleen was faithful to take the next step and go abroad to reach the nations. In Clarkston and the surrounding areas, our team had trained and partnered with many nationals who had language and culture from their homeland. We wanted to continue that partnership with them in going to the nations.

An opportunity was presented to us to partner with some nationals in Myanmar. When Colleen heard of this opportunity, she immediately felt a calling to go to Myanmar (formerly known as Burma). On the other hand, I did not feel called to go. Even though I was not called, I could tell that God had stirred Colleen's heart to go. It was a big step as we were lacking the finances and there was not a lot of time to prepare for the trip. Completing all the logistics in less than a month seemed to be a tall order. Colleen did feel a sense of urgency. We prayed that if God wanted her to go in such a short time, He would open the door and that He would provide the financing and the preparation on such short notice.

Colleen decided to commit herself to going. Her decision to go increased her confidence dramatically. It was by faith that she said, "I'll go." Colleen was able to present the vision of reaching the lost in Myanmar to the Atlanta Vineyard Church. We had worshipped there and related to them as our church family. This Vineyard church was able to take up a one-time offering. Through their generous giving, they came up with more than half of the funds needed to go. That offering alone boosted Colleen's confidence that God would be the source of her provision.

Up to that point, she had been concerned about the finances. She now pushed forward with more confidence than ever. Her team worked on training issues and logistics to get her visa approved. Her visa was approved within days. Colleen relied on another source to get most of the balance of what she needed. Our home church and others gave financially. We felt incredibly blessed and encouraged that God was faithful and had provided the finances and more for the trip.

Before leaving, several of Colleen's Burmese friends made her a *longyi* as a send-off gift (this is the traditional sheet of cloth worn in Myanmar). Her Burmese friends were so excited to see her go. They talked with Colleen about someday going back to Myanmar and sharing the Gospel with their families and others. There seemed to be enormous potential for reaching Myanmar with the Gospel.

Colleen left for Myanmar for two weeks in April of 2019 to teach and strengthen believers in a discipleship school and orphanage. The team trained with the No Place Left (NPL) discipleship process.

I (Colleen) and the team arrived at Yangon, and we stayed in a hotel that evening and for the rest of the trip. This seemed strange to me, but it was a requirement of the government that all visitors must stay at a hotel. During the day, the trainings were held at an orphanage. The training had to be translated into two languages, so it was slow going. However, the training was successful because our team took their time to ensure that the nationals understood the heart of the NPL training.

Those who were trained went on outreach and were able to minister and share with about thirty families. Of that thirty families, twenty-five were open and asked for a follow-up. I was already making connections with others as I wore my *longyi* that my Burmese friends in Georgia had made for me. It was a great conversation starter and made connecting with others easier.

I went out with the director of the orphanage and the discipleship school on Easter Sunday—an Easter I will never forget. The director took me to see several families who lived in the city dump. She specifically wanted us to meet an older gentleman who was previously bed-ridden. The director had visited with him, and she started praying in the name of Jesus for physical healing. He started praying on his own in the name of Jesus.

After praying, he was restored physically and was able to get out of bed. The director wanted me to meet with him and continue the good work God had started. We shared the Gospel with him and his family. We prayed for the entire family. He accepted Christ and was restored spiritually. He was a living testimony of Christ's changing power. As a result, he wanted a Bible. We gave him a Burmese Bible so he could read the Bible daily with his family.

Another family welcomed us into their home and listened as we shared a testimony and the story of the Samaritan woman (Luke 4:7–29). They did not accept Christ as their Savior at that time, but they were interested in learning more about Jesus.

A third family was happy to talk with us also. After sharing, the husband and the wife wanted to follow Jesus and they prayed for salvation. They were fearful about the living conditions as the rainy season was quickly approaching and would bring water and trash into their house. We prayed for protection from the water and asked God to bless the husband with a job, so they could move out of the dump.

As we were visiting with this family, a neighbor walked in and started listening to our conversation. When we were finished, he invited us to visit his house. Upon visiting his house, I noticed his wife was talking to a woman Buddhist monk. The monk quickly left, as we could see she was extremely uncomfortable. The husband was very hospitable and offered us tea. He was excited that we accepted his invitation. He had a lot of questions about Jesus. After we shared, he wanted to accept Christ as his Savior.

God used a single contact to reach many others through that relational network. I was completely amazed at how one contact had led to so many fruitful contacts. That is the true power of God. Some of these families could not leave to go to church so we suggested their house become a gathering place to worship the Lord. Two gatherings started at the dump, and within a couple of months, there were twenty-seven small-group gatherings in the surrounding areas. From the dump (a place of desolation and hopelessness) came life. Multiplication was happening at an incredible rate.

I was surprised at how open the people were to the Gospel and how easily several gatherings started. I expected much more resistance. God was on the move to engage nonbelievers and the existing believers were being strengthened and empowered by the growth of others coming to Christ.

Growth was happening at such a fast rate that the initial leaders who started the movement could not keep up. They needed more help and wanted additional training for new leaders. A second team followed up with the initial leaders and trained others to pick up the slack.

God was faithful to get the job done, despite the extreme heat and becoming sick. The heat was extreme (it was 106 degrees outdoors and 120-plus indoors.). I felt so sick that I wanted to die. God provided some medication which gave me much-needed relief. I asked our pray-support team in the United States to continue to pray about the heat and for a complete recovery from my illness. Shortly afterward, a fresh wind blew through the windows. The coolness of the breeze was so refreshing. It lifted all our spirits, and with God's help, I was able to persevere and accomplish what I needed to do.

I saw the hand of God at almost every turn. It was a humbling experience as well as an enriching one. I was willing to be available and take a risk. I am usually not a risk-taker. This was a big step for me and helped to deepen my faith in Christ. God was willing to help me to endure hardship to accomplish His will. Praise be to the Father.

Training and partnering with nationals helped to share the peace of the Gospel to people that might not otherwise get the chance to hear about such peace. Nationals were now catching the idea that God's heart was for all the nations. His heart is to truly reach every people group. By training and partnering with nationals who have culture and language, the Gospel was now clearing some of the hurdles that hindered it from going forward. I was so surprised at how open people were to the Gospel and that several gatherings had been started so easily.

After returning from Myanmar, Colleen and I reengaged with our team in Clarkston. I sensed a change of direction and so did Colleen. We prayed and our focus for the spring and summer of 2019 changed dramatically.

Our team leader had been praying and sensed a need to start working with youth. He saw that we needed to strengthen and encourage some youth in Clarkston. We were hoping that some of these youth might be interested in engaging people of their own culture and/or similar culture. We did not know who or where to start. Our whole team noticed many problems with the youth and families, but we were at a loss about who these youth might be. Our team began to pray more about this.

We saw technology as a major problem as the youth seemed to have access to all kinds of video games and other questionable material. They did not seem to have any restraints in this area. We could also see there was a shift of responsibility from the refugee parents to the kids, as the kids had learned English and how to navigate the US culture. The adults now relied on their children to help them. Some of the adults were not learning English or only knew a little. Some had not adjusted to the culture and remained isolated. The kids, on the other hand, were in school and were learning the English language and how to navigate in a new culture. Now the kids were acting as adults, and it was a complete role reversal. We were seeing these things but still had questions. We still did not know which youth and how many we would be working with. We continued to pray.

Our team leader worked hard to make contacts. It was slow going and there was not much of a response. We continued to pray that we would get connected with some youth that were hungry and ready to respond. We wanted quality versus quantity. We prayed about this a lot.

We were finally able to start working with four Burmese youth who had a heart for the Lord and were hungry for more. One of them had been praying for something more than just going to summer camp. She was so glad to join us. All of them caught the idea that God loved them. They also caught the idea that they wanted to serve God, not out of obligation but because of His great love for them.

Each of them were at different levels of their faith walk. There were a lot of questions about faith issues and what it meant to serve and obey Christ. We started working with these four youth by meeting with them three times a week. We spent anywhere from thirteen to sixteen hours a week doing life-on-life. We ate together, prayed together, trained together, read the Bible, worshipped, and did outreach together.

Due to all our crazy schedules, not all of us were available to teach or train the whole summer. God gave us grace so that someone was always available to teach or train every time we met. That was one of the many benefits of team teaching. We all had confidence in each other and did not miss a beat. It was so amazing to see them grow in the Lord and start to ask the harder questions. In turn, we were able to learn so much from them; we were learners again. We discovered firsthand the struggles and issues that they faced. We also learned about Burmese youth-culture lingo and the like. We found out about the clash of cultures that they experience when they come to the United States. It was a growing experience for us as well as for them.

One other benefit was that our team grew closer as we spent more time together. We felt as though we knew each other on a deeper level. We felt more confident that it was God working instead of us individually.

The summer discipleship experience gave us valuable insight into how to engage youth, as this was a totally new area for us. We saw the benefit of taking them out for evangelism due to their cultural connection and language abilities. The language connection was awesome, as this was one more answered prayer for the language barrier.

I remembered our many prayers for guidance about how to overcome the language barrier. God was faithful. God was not going to be thwarted by a lack of a common language that created a barrier. He was reaching the nations as He promised He would. As I looked at the book of Revelation, I truly saw God working His plan to be faithful and bring glory to Himself. He was using different cultures of mankind to someday bring them all together to bow down to Him and to worship Him. Praise be to the Father.

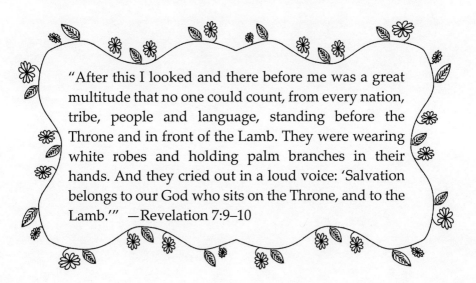

"After this I looked and there before me was a great multitude that no one could count, from every nation, tribe, people and language, standing before the Throne and in front of the Lamb. They were wearing white robes and holding palm branches in their hands. And they cried out in a loud voice: 'Salvation belongs to our God who sits on the Throne, and to the Lamb.'" —Revelation 7:9–10

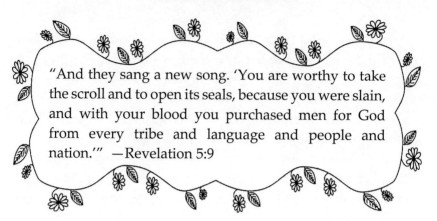

"And they sang a new song. 'You are worthy to take the scroll and to open its seals, because you were slain, and with your blood you purchased men for God from every tribe and language and people and nation.'" —Revelation 5:9

15

Change Is in the Air

O ne of the things that I did not anticipate was how important technology is becoming to reach people with the Gospel. Most of us either hate it or love it. However, no matter what our position, the impact cannot be denied.

For me, "technology" was a bad word as I saw so many flaws and problems that it created. I am old school and have not adapted well to this change. Relationships are more key to me. Personal interaction is paramount in developing relationships. However, it is nice to have things at your fingertips. Information can make our life simple, and information can now be exchanged in a flash. The problem is that technology has now created an environment where it is hard to discern the truth. I have labeled the age we live in as the "Age of Misinformation." When people put their identity and/or personal information on social media, it can be harmful. Also, because of the misinformation, trust is difficult to establish. When a person's identity is found in anything but Jesus, there will be issues.

Despite the problems with technology, God will not be thwarted in achieving His goals. Time and time again, we have seen that people respond better when they can read or hear something in their native tongue or language.

We have a friend who trained us on how to use this technology to get God's Word to people. He was able to develop a mobile Wi-Fi system that could send a copy of the Bible to someone's phone or tablet. This is nothing new; the new development is that he used technology to send this information to someone's phone or tablet without using their own Wi-Fi or data. Now, the film about Jesus or other Christian digital information can be sent directly to someone's personal electronic device.

These Wi-Fi boxes are now available for distribution and can be used anywhere. Numerous times, we had problems communicating, especially on a deeper level, due to the language barrier. This new technology helped us to overcome that barrier. Sharing the film about Jesus with others is as simple as putting their number in a phone and then sending the information to them. They can then have it translated into their heart language so that they are able to read and understand the Word of God. They now have a choice presented to them. For those who cannot read, this technology is also available in video format. This allows people to see and hear the Word of God. The availability of the Gospel now seems limitless. One more prayer answered about the language barrier. We began seeing the impact of technology and how important it is becoming to reach people with the Gospel. There now seemed to be a connection with people that we did not have before.

One other important avenue of technology is that we are all becoming more connected on a worldwide basis. As social media and the internet have become the norm for sharing information, more people than ever are connecting on a worldwide basis. Some are sharing their faith through various social platforms. Social media is changing the information flow, and now, more people than ever have the Gospel at their fingertips. People are reaching the nations without leaving the comfort of their own living rooms.

Technology is changing the way we live and do business. It is definitively changing the way the Gospel is getting to others. I have seen people's faces come to life when they were able to read or hear the Bible in their own language. Many have never seen or heard the Word of God until they were able to hear or read it in their own native language. The Word of God is now being heard and seen in a new light, and it is making a huge difference.

I envision a day when we will be able to use technology to communicate with most people throughout the world. I envision a day when I will be able to speak English and it will be translated into thousands of viable languages. That technology is already here, it is just a matter of developing a system to market it to the masses. As the whole earth is becoming more connected, I can see more people than ever being influenced by the Gospel.

I know that Christians are making an impact with technology. When I went to my first missions conference in 2013, there were approximately 16,500 unreached people groups in the world; today, there are 7,298 unreached people groups (according to the Joshua Project).[1] Wycliffe Bible Translators USA has translated the complete Bible into 698 languages. Wycliffe has translated at least some portion of the Bible into 3,384 languages.[2] Even so, there remains 6,665 languages (as of 2020) that do not have any Bible translation.[3] I believe technology will play a major role in reaching the remaining unreached people groups.

The real story is, God will use technology or any other means at His disposal. In Jesus's day, there were approximately seven million Jews (two million in Palestine and five million scattered elsewhere). One hundred twenty Jews gathered in the upper room, which represented .000017%, an exceedingly small percentage of the Jewish people. In a matter of days, after Pentecost, these disciples went out and shared their faith and this new community began growing by the thousands. There were six church-planting movements in the book of Acts, in which millions of people were engaged in less than fifteen years. This movement was later accused of turning the world upside down.

Technology was changing the landscape, but Colleen and I sensed there were other changes on the horizon. Changes can be hard, but they are needed to move us forward, to keep us fresh.

---

[1] https://joshuaproject.net/people_groups/statistics.
[2] https://www.wycliffe.org/about/why.
[3] Wycliffe Bible Translators USA, p. 188.

We often resist change and see it in a negative light. We tend to resist change as we are creatures of habit. Habits lock us into being comfortable. Change causes us to feel uncomfortable. However, change forces us out of our comfort zone and creates growth.

Colleen and I had been praying and sensed that big changes were coming. The Vineyard of Atlanta had picked up on this theme as well and had been praying for us. As usual, I had many questions. I always seem to. One of the things that I noticed was that No Place Left was a great place to get started, but I wanted to see disciples move through the intermediate and long-term discipleship process. I knew the tools were available to help move disciples along with personal growth, but we were not seeing that level of growth.

Personally, I sensed a need to go deeper in the Word. It was clear to me that, as Christians, we need to move from spiritual milk to meat. Christians need to understand God's Word better so it can be learned, obeyed, and then taught. It struck me as quite odd that most of what I was learning from No Place Left training was not being taught in churches. I realized this present church generation knows less about the Bible than the previous generations. Sharing their faith with others seems to be less important. With some, issues of faith were completely a personal issue. Many have not been exposed to or even understand the Great Commission. I am hoping to take what was started with No Place Left and build upon it. The Bible teaches and gives us a compass for learning how to live our lives.

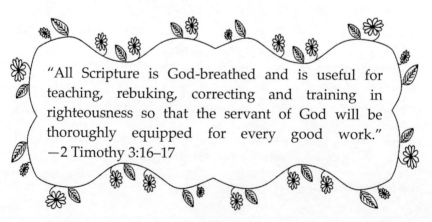

"All Scripture is God-breathed and is useful for teaching, rebuking, correcting and training in righteousness so that the servant of God will be thoroughly equipped for every good work."
—2 Timothy 3:16–17

What did that mean specifically for me? As I was pondering this thought, I was invited to an orientation at the Clarkston Bible Institute (CBI). The institute offered training that would cover Bible interpretation, preaching, theological issues, Old and New Testament surveys, church history, and much more. The course would last about one year and would prepare leaders and/or pastors to be more effective in ministry. I went to the orientation, and I prayed about the next step.

As the classes would start in one week, I needed to decide quickly. It would be a dramatic change and I knew it would be hard work. I had not been in school for over thirty-three years. There would be a lot of reading and studying as the class would cover the basics of the Bible from cover to cover. It would certainly add some depth to what we were currently doing. I prayed about this, as I did not have the tuition and it would affect available ministry time. I decided to attend CBI and move to the next level of my faith. We had a great class of students as well as top-notch teachers. The class was one of the biggest to date and the most diverse. It was just the thing I needed to start going deeper. It was just the beginning of things to come.

More changes were coming. Colleen's mother had fallen and suffered some injuries. She broke her arm and received a concussion. She was hospitalized and she also started to develop a heart problem. Colleen decided to go to Pennsylvania to help her mother recover and continue fundraising efforts in Ohio. It was a long separation of almost four months. I continued with my studies at CBI and enjoyed the teachings and fellowship with the other students.

After Colleen returned from Pennsylvania, my father went into the hospital and needed our attention. Back to Ohio, we went, for about a month. It was quite an ordeal, as my dad was hospitalized twice and was sent to rehab twice. God gave us patience to help my dad navigate the medical system and get him on the road to recovery. Family visited Dad during this time, and he began to see how important that connection would be to continue his recovery.

My dad was amazed at how many prayer-lists he was on. Knowing that so many were praying for him and us made all the difference. It was amazing to see how God used this difficult situation to motivate my dad to begin the process of selling his house and moving closer to family and church fellowship in Ohio.

When we returned to Clarkston, we encountered another difficult situation. One of my classmates from CBI had been in and out of the hospital for several months. She had internal bleeding, and no one seemed to be able to figure out why. Colleen and I prayed, as well as all my classmates. We visited with our friend at the hospital to try and encourage her. She had cancer throughout her body, and she appeared very weak and tired. The future for her life seemed uncertain but she was still looking for what the Lord's next mission was for her. We were glad to meet her family as many of them were Christians and believed in the power of prayer.

As we saw her condition deteriorate, we grieved with her family. However, she was a living testimony that she could face the unknown because her name was written in the Book of Life. She knew that whatever she might face, God would be with her. Christ had certainly made a difference in her life as He had given her peace to face the unknown. Her strength and courage helped renew and revitalize our faith as well as many others.

Our beloved friend would finally succumb to cancer. Her death brought us back to the reality that life is short. There are no easy answers when it comes to someone dying. I believe her confidence in Christ was a living testimony for everyone she met. We prayed for her family and friends and that they could somehow look beyond the pain of this world. Our hope was that God would reveal Himself during their time of loss. We also prayed that our friend's confidence in Christ was a light that directed others to see their need for Christ.

For Colleen and me, getting back in the swing of things was a difficult process as we faced further difficulties and challenges. One of the biggest challenges came from the COVID-19 virus and the fallout. The virus created major disruptions and problems worldwide. As the virus continued to spread, day-to-day activities were changed in ways that seemed unimaginable. The world was altered dramatically within just a few weeks. Most everything was shut down and, depending on where you lived, a complete lockdown was ordered. Social distancing, wearing masks, and video conferencing became the norm. Hoarding became an issue, as fear seemed to rule the day.

Food became scarce and prices skyrocketed. People were being evicted left and right due to the economic downturn. People became isolated from each other, and misinformation seemed to abound. As the world had been turned on its ear, many were seeing the economic fallout from the virus. The number of cases and deaths continued to rise daily. There were a lot of questions. *Would we ever return to normal? What would the landscape look like from the fallout of the virus? When will the stay-at-home orders be lifted?*

There were more questions than answers. Sports, entertainment, going wherever we wanted, economic growth, and community were just some of the causalities. Almost in an instant, the options that we took for granted disappeared. Many were suffering and, due to social distancing, could not be with their loved ones. Many were mourning the death of a family member or friend and could not attend the funeral. Hospitalizations were another problem, as families were being denied access to visit their loved ones. Mental health issues were increasing, and violence began erupting around the world. Every sound bite seemed to be about the virus and the increased violence.

There were many more issues that continued to crop up that no one had anticipated. The pandemic and increase in violence were causing worldwide havoc, and the prospects of improvement did not look good. People were hoping the government could step in and save the day, but it was apparent these tragedies transcended man's ability to solve them. Many began to see their normal way of life fading away fast.

Despite the doom and gloom and the conspiracy theories, the

bigger picture is that God was the same before the COVID-19 virus and increased violence and He will still be the same during and after it. Keeping everything in perspective, the church needed to think outside the box to continue fellowshipping and address COVID-19 and race issues. Unfortunately, social distancing and other safety measures seemed to be a part of our future for quite some time. Video meetings and other communication applications allowed many to still stay connected during the crisis but in an entirely new way.

Through all the chaos, the church was still the church, building or no building, face to face or not. Even though this became a difficult time for all, the community of believers stood out as a light to all those who were losing hope. Christians were being called to give an account of the hope that was in them despite the dire circumstances faced. We continue to pray that people will turn to God in their time of need and seek His face during this uncertain and unprecedented time. We also pray that the believers in Christ will reach out to any neighbor in need and be the light and salt of the earth. The church has long known that God does not delight in man's troubles.

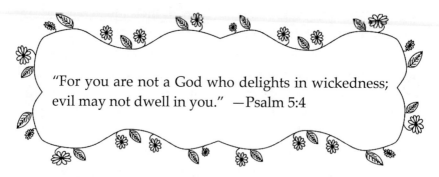

"For you are not a God who delights in wickedness; evil may not dwell in you." —Psalm 5:4

God also shows people that there is nothing new under the sun and that the things we see now have happened in the past.

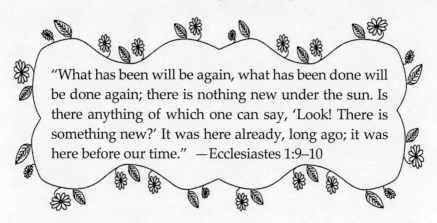

"What has been will be again, what has been done will be done again; there is nothing new under the sun. Is there anything of which one can say, 'Look! There is something new?' It was here already, long ago; it was here before our time." —Ecclesiastes 1:9–10

There have been pandemics that have killed millions. There have been natural disasters of all kinds in world history. Wars, strife, racism, economic collapses, and the list goes on. The real question is, how are we going to respond to such things? God is calling us to Him in full dependence because He knows we will face such things as history continues to repeat itself. Life will have difficulties and challenges.

However, God is also calling us to Him through salvation in Christ when there will be a day that all our tears will be wiped away. There will be no more pain or suffering. As Christians, we look forward to that time. While we wait and watch, we are to be engaged in effectively ministering to others for His name's sake. We remain confident that God will use us to continue making his name known to all nations.

16

To All the Nations

As I move forward, I see Revelation 7:9–10 in the future. Maybe even in my lifetime.

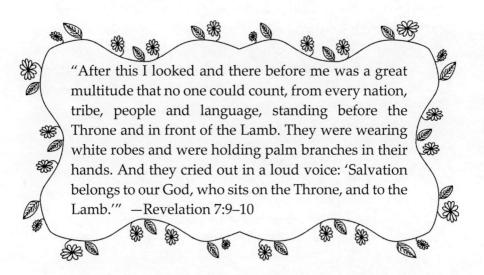

"After this I looked and there before me was a great multitude that no one could count, from every nation, tribe, people and language, standing before the Throne and in front of the Lamb. They were wearing white robes and were holding palm branches in their hands. And they cried out in a loud voice: 'Salvation belongs to our God, who sits on the Throne, and to the Lamb.'" —Revelation 7:9–10

There is going to be unity in diversity. God in His very nature is so diverse. His complexity is beyond measure and beyond the scope of human understanding. Yet God remains with us and is a personal God who is concerned about every area of our lives. God will use extraordinary means to reach his people. God is working on His master plan to see that all nations hear about His name. All different people groups will come together to worship the Lord.

They will be from every nation (*ethnos*: Greek for people group), tribe, people, and language. It is because God is faithful, and His Word is true. It is because He works in community with Himself and through a community of believers. He will see that His name is glorified and worshipped. God is with us in community and that cannot be overemphasized.

As believers, our desire should not be about whether people are going to heaven or hell. It should not be a checklist of dos and don'ts. It should not be about trying to convert others. Our life-long goal should be getting to know Jesus and showing that type of love to others. Growing in the knowledge of Jesus Christ is maturing in the faith. It only happens in community. In communion with God and then other believers who bear His image.

This is the Gospel of peace: to share the truth, in community with others, that a relationship that was once broken can be restored through Jesus and what He did at the Cross. The power of the Gospel is that He not only died for our sins, but He rose from the dead. Christ broke the power of sin and death that we are all under. This is not only the "Good News," it is the "Best News." God stepped into our world first. Sin and its effects can be taken off the table if we turn from our sin and put our faith and trust in Jesus.

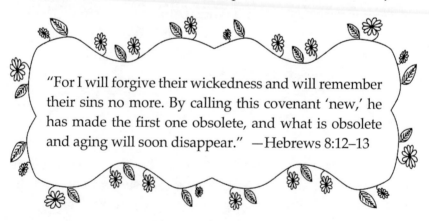

"For I will forgive their wickedness and will remember their sins no more. By calling this covenant 'new,' he has made the first one obsolete, and what is obsolete and aging will soon disappear." —Hebrews 8:12–13

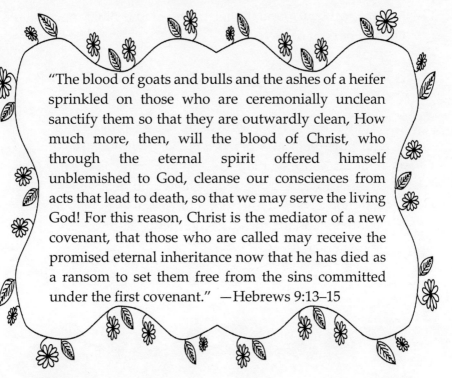

"The blood of goats and bulls and the ashes of a heifer sprinkled on those who are ceremonially unclean sanctify them so that they are outwardly clean, How much more, then, will the blood of Christ, who through the eternal spirit offered himself unblemished to God, cleanse our consciences from acts that lead to death, so that we may serve the living God! For this reason, Christ is the mediator of a new covenant, that those who are called may receive the promised eternal inheritance now that he has died as a ransom to set them free from the sins committed under the first covenant." —Hebrews 9:13–15

My prayer is that you do not just take my word for it. Pick up the Bible and begin reading it for yourself. I challenge you to become a truth-seeker and ask God to help you find the truth. God is love, and the greatest, most loving act of all time was to provide a plan of reconciliation to Himself for all sinful humanity.

Mankind has a myriad of problems, but there is only one solution. It is the name of Jesus that is above all else and is greatly to be praised. My prayer is that you seek Christ's righteousness through the Cross and His shed blood for your sins. Be like the Bereans in the seventeenth chapter in the book of Acts who were of noble character, received the Word with great eagerness, and were willing to read the Scriptures daily to test the authenticity of what they heard. They also did it all in community.

Furthermore, my hope is that you begin to love God with all your heart, soul, mind, and strength and then begin to love people. To be on a mission with God and His community to build a foundation on the Rock. As you begin to build on the Rock, you will want to obey foundational truths of the Bible, not out of obligation but out of love.

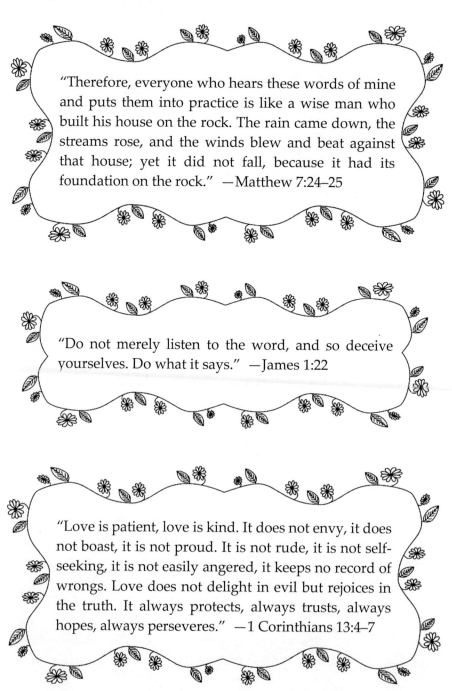

"Therefore, everyone who hears these words of mine and puts them into practice is like a wise man who built his house on the rock. The rain came down, the streams rose, and the winds blew and beat against that house; yet it did not fall, because it had its foundation on the rock." —Matthew 7:24–25

"Do not merely listen to the word, and so deceive yourselves. Do what it says." —James 1:22

"Love is patient, love is kind. It does not envy, it does not boast, it is not proud. It is not rude, it is not self-seeking, it is not easily angered, it keeps no record of wrongs. Love does not delight in evil but rejoices in the truth. It always protects, always trusts, always hopes, always perseveres." —1 Corinthians 13:4–7

Acknowledgments

Thanks to all those who have supported Colleen and me with their finances and prayers over the years. Thanks also for the many communities we have met that have truly enriched our lives beyond measure and given us a glimpse of God that would not be possible without them. We remain eternally grateful and thankful to our Heavenly Father. Without Him and community, this endeavor would be impossible.

Praise and thanks to the Father, Son, and Holy Spirit. Amen. Thanks also for the many who encouraged us with this endeavor with their prayers, finances, words of support, technical support, and hope.

We wanted to express our gratitude to God for our friend and fellow coworker for the Kingdom of God. He suddenly passed away on July 13, 2020. Delynn Hoover's vision for discipleship has touched our lives and the lives of thousands whom he passionately served in Latin America and the United States.

Special thanks to Matt Leveille and Gene Smarr for helping edit the text and to Ted Hatfield for computer technical support. Thanks also to Globe International as our supporting agency in ministry efforts.

About the Authors

Armin and Colleen have been married thirty-one years and have two married sons and one daughter. They are missionaries with Globe International Ministries and started their missionary journey in 2008, taking them to four of the seven continents. Currently, they serve in Clarkston, Georgia, ministering to refugees, internationals, and Americans by teaching evangelism and discipleship by living life-on-life with God and His people.